The Bawdy House Girls

A Look at the Brothels of the Old West

By Alton Pryor

The Bawdy House Girls

A Look at the Brothels of the Old West

By Alton Pryor

The Bawdy House Girls

A Look at the Brothels of the Old West

Copyright © 2006 Alton Pryor

ISBN: 0-9747551-7-6

Library of Congress Control No.: 2006900022

First Printing 2006

Stagecoach Publishing
5360 Campcreek Loop
Roseville, CA. 95747
stagecoach@surewest.net
www.stagecoachpublishing.com

Wherever there's civilization and a newspaper, there will be a police blotter. Here's an unpleasant entry:

Carrie "Spring Chicken" Smith, notorious Truckee (California) prostitute, took a dose of morphine. She was in jail in Virginia City for assault and battery. Later in the month she tried to hang herself with a hanky.

Table of Contents

The Arm of the Law

Introduction

Entertainment in the early cowtowns was more important than religion. It is told of a man who went on a mission to raise funds to build a church, but later he changed his mind, and built a dance hall. He was obviously hungrier for entertainment than religion.

To fill the western dance halls, women often traveled to eastern cities in search of girls. Young girls who may never have considered prostitution were over-powered by the allure of promised riches.

They were told of the possibilities of landing a rich husband if they would simply make the trip.

The life of a prostitute, in most cases, did not last long. Many of the women took their own lives or lived on the streets after their parlor-house careers were finished.

In some cases, action was not taken against the prostitutes, madams, and the houses in which they worked because the prominent people in town supported them. The houses of prostitution were very good for a town's economy.

Chapter 1

Mattie Silks

Mattie Silks made one thing clear. She did not work as a prostitute.

She was Colorado's most successful madam, and proud of it. She was a businesswoman first and the madam of a posh whorehouse second, but she did not turn tricks herself.

Mattie enforced a firm rule. "I never took a girl into my house who had had no previous experience of life and men. That was a rule of mine. No innocent young girl was ever hired by me. And they came to me for

Mattie Silks
(Google Images)

the same reasons that I hired them. Because there was money in it for all of us."

Mattie opened her house in Denver to attract the silver and gold prospectors raging in the state

13

at the time. Her house was a three-story brick mansion with 27 rooms, including 16 bedrooms, 4 parlors, and a ballroom with a 16-foot round mirror set in the ceiling.

A trip upstairs with one of Mattie's girls cost anywhere from ten dollars to two-hundred-dollars. On a ten-dollar trick, Mattie kept four-dollars.

Mattie insisted that all her men customers be treated as gentlemen. The girls were allowed to sit only on the ottomans scattered around the parlor area, not on the chairs and never on the laps of the male guests.

The rule was, "Be a lady in the drawing room and a whore in the bedroom." Once the doors were closed it was "anything goes."

One madam that practiced her trade in both Texas and Oklahoma, described the business. "I've laid it in all of 'em. I throwed my fanny twenty-one times a night, five bucks a throw and by the time old red-eye come up, I was eatin' breakfast drunker'n an Indian."

Mattie is thought to have been born in Terre Haute, or perhaps Gary, Indiana, 1846 to 1848, and to have run away from home at age thirteen. Her given name is not recorded, but on certain documents pertaining to her, including her death certificate, the first name Martha was used.

According to Clark Secrest, in his *Hell's Belles, Prostitution, Vice, and Crime in Early Denver,* an envelope found under the flooring of one of her Market Street houses was addressed to "Miss Maté Weinman." She is not known to have ever used that name.

Her death certificate asserted that her father and mother were unknown.

At age nineteen, in Springfield, Illinois, Mattie opened her first "sporting house". She maintained she had never been a prostitute herself and bragged that she was unique in this respect.

She told Janie Green, another Denver madam, that she had recruited three girls from Abilene, Kansas, and one from Dodge City, and headed west. Her new employees worked from a tent along the way.

With the tent as a traveling bordello, Mattie and her four girls headed for the Colorado mountains, carrying along the first portable bathtub to enter the mining camps. Their initial stop was Jamestown, northwest of Boulder.

From there, Mattie proceeded to Georgetown, where she met Cort Thomson. It was apparently at the same time she ran her Springfield brothel back in Illinois in 1864 that she coined the name of "Silks" for a last name.

She adopted it because of her love for silk materials. Little or nothing is known of her childhood. She died without revealing any of the secrets of her early years, including her true name.

The gold and silver mines of Colorado were literally pouring rich ore out of its veins and *The Bawdy House Girls* were raking it in as fast as the miners could dig it out of the ground.

In Denver, the cribs operated by the prostitutes were little different from the red light districts of other gold rush towns. These cribs were lined up shoulder-to-shoulder and were barely wide enough for a door and a front window.

The standard rental for such a place was twenty-five dollars a week, paid in advance. It is here that the street-walkers and the one-dollar whores hung out. The going rate was one-dollar if the girl was white and four-bits if she was black.

Madams operating the fancy parlor houses forbid their girls from associating with the crib girls. This was to justify their higher prices. The parlor house madams wanted their clientele to understand their merchandise was higher quality.

In Georgetown, Colorado, Mattie Silks operated one of the five parlor houses on Brownell Street. The area was described as "the richest square mile on earth." It was likewise the source of Mattie Silks' great wealth.

It was in Georgetown that Mattie met the love of her life, a handsome Texan by the name of Cortese D. Thomson. While he was handsome, lithe and lean, Thomson was also a sponger of the worst type.

Thomson was a professional "foot racer", a sporting event that once attracted gamblers by the droves. The sport was fading fast at the time that Mattie met her man.

Even though Thomson spent Mattie's money as fast he could convince her to give it to him, she still worshiped him. While Mattie was not bad looking, she was rather short and always appeared "overweight".

Mattie's consort, the handsome Cort Thomson, (middle row, seated, without striped stockings, organized foot-racing contests between volunteer fire departments.

(Colorado Historical Society)

The handsome "Cort" was not only tall, but a few years younger than Mattie. She considered him a real prize.

Some estimates figure Mattie doled out as much as seventy-five-thousand dollars to Cort, which he lost gambling and playing the big spender. He also cheated on Mattie.

In 1876, Mattie moved from Georgetown to Denver. Cort, naturally, accompanied her as she was his own personal money source.

Mattie Silks, left, with the pride of her racing stable, Jim Blaine. (Denver Library, Western Collection)

Her first property in Denver was 501 McGaa Street, which she occupied for years. She brought in twelve young and good looking "boarders" to occupy the many rooms in the house.

Mattie's parlor house of twelve *bawdy* girls did so well she invested in another. This one she rented out to Jennie Rogers, a dashing brunette that had the elegance that Mattie desired but could never achieve.

While Mattie loved expensive silks, her taste in clothes was pitiful, even though costly. Her costumes appeared Victorian and almost comical rather than stylish.

When Mattie and Cort returned from a trip to Europe, they found Denver and its red light district virtually deserted. The gold rush had moved to

Alaska and the Yukon. A rich gold strike had been made in the Klondike.

Mattie and Cort moved with the strike, taking along her bevy of twelve boarders. Mattie rented a house for four-hundred dollars a month in Dawson, and paid fifty dollars a day in protection to the Dawson police.

She had never made so much money so quickly as she did in Dawson. Still, the weather was atrocious and she feared Cort was catching pneumonia. She decided to pull up stakes and return to Denver. She reopened her Denver parlor.

Because Cort was drinking too much, Mattie wanted to get him away from town and the temptations of alcohol. With financing from Mattie, Cort bought three pieces of land in the little town of Wray, east of Denver.

It wasn't long before his neighbors were accusing him of running off their stock and altering the brands. When Mattie visited Cort, she immediately disliked the way Cort was operating.

She discharged Cort's foreman, a man known locally as Dirty Face Murphy, and hired in his place Jack Ready, a tall and handsome mountain of a man.

Cort became ill. A doctor diagnosed the cause as a severe attack of stomach cramps, caused by cirrhosis of the liver and excessive drinking. He gave Mattie a bottle of laudanum, and suggested she lace Cort's whiskey with it as needed.

Mattie followed the doctors orders throughout the night, but at daybreak, Cort was pronounced dead.

Mattie soon married Jack Ready, the manager of her ranch property. He acted as her bookkeeper and bouncer for the drunks who frequently staggered into the house during the night.

Ready remained with Mattie through the years. She died in 1929 at the age of eighty-three.

Chapter 2

Julia Bulette

She was just a prostitute in the bustling gold camp of Virginia City, Nevada, but she was a respected one.

For Virginia Engine Company No. 1, Virginia City's volunteer fire department, "Jule" Bulette was special. She worked the brakes when the firemen went on calls. She was an honorary member of the firemen's brigade.

Virginia City was born by the discovery of the Comstock Mine. Saloons sprouted faster than did miner's tents. And as soon as there was a saloon or a boarding house opened, it

Julia Bulette, a Virginia City favorite.
(Google Images)

usually had prostitutes and dance-hall girls ready to give pleasure to the miners, all for a price.

21

Makeshift "cribs" sprang up along "D" Street in Virginia City. There were "high-class" prostitutes, simple streetwalkers, and women that had succumbed to alcohol or drug addiction, all trying to get their pinch of gold dust from the miner's poke.

One section of "C" street was called "The Barbary Coast," adapted from the famous Barbary Coast in San Francisco. In a short time, the Barbary Coast in Virginia City was said to be twice as evil as the one in San Francisco.

In 1863, Virginia City's Board of Aldermen passed an ordinance against houses of prostitution in an effort to cut down the lawlessness and debauchery attached to them.

The Virginia Evening Bulletin reported:

> *The Board of Aldermen, at their meeting on the 13th, took action upon the many nuisances at present existing in our midst in the shape of houses of ill fame, and passed a stringent ordinance against their existence in so central a part of town.*
>
> *We are glad to see the Board have some regard for the morality of the city, and their recent action has met the hearty approval of our citizens.*
>
> *The first section of the ordinance says that it shall be unlawful to open or maintain any house of ill-repute or brothel in the district of this city west of D street, or south of Sutton Avenue*

or north of Mill street; and the second section sets forth that any owner of a house or property included in the district in this city who shall let, hire or rent his or her property for the occupancy of women of bad or immoral character, shall give and pay to the city five hundred dollars. Some may consider this rather stringent, but we do not, and we hope to see the provisions of the ordinance carried into effect.

The ordinance was hardly passed when a fire swept through the area, destroying a number of buildings occupied by prostitutes. The ladies simply moved to other quarters outside the restricted area.

In 1874, The Virginia and Truckee Railroad Company purchased the burned out property to continue their railroad and to build a depot. The company graded the property to locate warehouses, depot premises and sidetracks.

The prostitutes that were still in the area were warned to vacate their houses or be plowed under, but many stayed, rent free, until the last moment. They always found new buildings to occupy and carry on their trade.

The citizens continued to complain about the lewd women and shameless men occupying the dens of inequity in their midst but other than an occasional arrest, little was done to move the ladies of the evening out of town.

Virginia City in the 1870 era.   (Mark Twain Bookstore)

Julia Bulette's background is a bit obscured by a number of historical fallacies.

It is believed she was born in London, but immigrated to New Orleans at a very young age. Details are sparse, and some historians claim she was married there to a man named "Smith". Whether real or fictional, she was separated from him and traveled to California in 1852. Settling first in the town of Weaverville, she worked as a prostitute before moving to Virginia City in 1863.

Some writers trifle even more with her background, claiming she was a mulatto born in Natchez, Mississippi and worked as a prostitute in

New Orleans. Guy Rocha, Nevada State archivist dispels that as complete fiction.

Rocha says contrary to some writers, Julia never wore silk, velvet and sable furs. Neither was she making one thousand dollars a night for her services, and she was not accepting gold bars of bullion, diamonds or rubies as payment.

"She was neither wealthy, beautiful, willowy, nor did the rather heavy-set woman seemingly float when she walked," Rocha says, declaring much of what was written about her was myth.

What is true is that Julia met a horrible death at thirty seven years of age. She was strangled and clubbed with the hammer of a pistol while laying in bed.

About 11:30 p.m. Saturday, January 18, Julia said goodnight to her next door neighbor, Gertrude Holmes (also a prostitute), telling her she had to meet a miner that was coming to see her.

At 11 a.m., Sunday, a Chinese houseboy came in and built a fire but was careful not to disturb her, thinking she was asleep. At 11:30, her body was discovered by her friend Gertrude, who came to call her to breakfast.

The bed covers on either side of the body were not disturbed, so it was obvious she had not shared the bed with anyone. A coroners report said she had been struck with the hammer of a pistol and beaten with an eighteen-inch stick of firewood.

Clear imprints of fingers and a thumb remained on her throat. Many of her finer pieces of jewelry and clothing were missing.

Julia was buried on Monday, the day following her death. Her funeral procession included the Metropolitan Brass Band, about sixty members of the volunteer fire department marching on foot, and sixteen carriages of mourners. Included were her friends among the sisterhood of prostitutes.

One thing that helped to solve her murder was the fact that the villain didn't leave town. Martha Camp, a friend of Julia's, was awakened by someone approaching her door. When she screamed, her attacker fled.

Martha, however, had gotten a clear view of the man. A short time later, she recognized him on the street and reported it to the police.

The man's name was Jean Marie A. Villain, a Frenchman that worked in a bakery on D street. Villain had adopted the name of John Millian. He spoke very little English.

A break in Julia Bulette's murder came from a Mrs. Cazentre, of Gold Hill, just outside of Virginia City. She told police she had purchased a dress that once belonged to Julia Bulette from John Millian for forty dollars. Millian told her he was selling the dress for a widow whose husband had been killed in the Ophir mine.

The dress was positively identified as belonging to Julia by dry goods merchant Sam Rosener, who said he sold the dress to Julia himself. He had acquired the entire shipment of that particular pattern when it arrived in San Francisco.

Millian, the accused, had also left a trunk in storage at the bakery where he worked. When the trunk was searched, nearly all of Julia's missing clothing and other items was inside.

A jury convicted Millian to hang. At 12:42 p.m., April 24, 1868, the killer was brought before three-thousand onlookers and marched up the gallows steps.

One man who returned to Virginia City to witness the execution was Mark Twain, who worked as a reporter for the *Territorial Enterprise* in Virginia City.

The *Gold Hill News* described the scene, in which Millian read his farewell address, claiming to the end that he was innocent. He claimed that the police chief had perjured himself on the witness stand, and abandoned women had been brought in to swear Millain's life away.

Julia Bulette's personal estate was sparse. The sale of her belongings brought eight-hundred-seventy-five dollars and forty-three-cents, while she owed seven-hundred-ninety-one-dollars.

Julia was considered just another prostitute, but at the same time, very much a kind woman.

Chapter 3

Big Nose Kate

Mary Katherine Haroney was born in well-to-do circumstances in Budapest, Hungary in 1850. Her father was a doctor. In 1865, Dr. Haroney was appointed personal surgeon to Mexico's Emperor Maximilian. The family moved to Mexico to fulfill the appointment.

Kate Haroney (seated) in her younger days with her sister.
(Google Images)

In 1865, Maximilian's rule crumbled, forcing the Haroney family to flee Mexico. They went to Davenport, Iowa, where her mother died while Kate was only fourteen. Her father died a short time after.

Kate and her siblings were placed in foster homes. When she was sixteen-years-old, Kate was put in the care of a man named Otto Smith. She was so displeased with the situation she soon ran away. Kate stowed aboard a steamship headed for St. Louis. The ship's captain found Kate, but he didn't put her off the boat.

Doc Holliday and Big Nose Kate.

(Google Images)

She was allowed to travel on to St. Louis. There, Kate assumed Captain Fisher's name and enrolled in a convent school in St. Louis.

If history is correct, Kate married a dentist, Silas Melvin. The couple had a child, but both her husband and the child died the same year.

In 1874 Kate worked in a *bawdy* house in Wichita, Kansas for Wyatt Earp's wife, Nellie Bessie Earp. A year later, Kate was using the name of Kate Elder and was listed in Dodge City, Kansas as a dance hall girl.

A fateful meeting occurred for Kate when she moved to Fort Griffin, Texas. There, dealing cards in John Shanssey's Saloon was John Henry "Doc" Holliday. Kate spent the next several years traveling the west with Holliday.

Their relationship was stormy at times. Kate was as tough, stubborn and hot-tempered as was

Holliday. When a domestic battle erupted, Kate didn't hesitate. She returned to being a prostitute.

Big Nose Kate's Saloon in Tombstone, Arizona.
(Google Images)

She said she worked the business because she liked it. She belonged to no man, nor to any house.

One night, Doc Holliday ran up against a problem in a card game he was dealing. A local bully named Ed Bailey picked up the discards and looked at them. This was strictly forbidden in western poker parlors. A violation of the rule could result in the player forfeiting the pot.

Holliday called Bailey on the violation twice. Bailey ignored him and did it a third time. Holliday reached out and raked the pot in without showing his hand.

Bailey brought out a gun, but before he fired, Holliday had a knife in his hand and slashed Bailey across the stomach. Blood spewed everywhere. Doc felt his actions were in self-defense and did not run. Holliday was arrested and, being the town had no jail, held for trial in a local hotel room. A vigilante group formed to deal with Holliday in their own way.

When Big Nose Kate heard of the situation, she plotted on how to free Holliday. She figured the mob would easily over-power the lawmen guarding Holliday, and lynch him for sure.

Kate set fire to an old shed. It's flames threatened to engulf the entire town. While everyone was scrambling to squelch the fire, Kate confronted Holliday's guard with a pistol in each hand, and disarmed him. She and Holliday escaped.

All that night they hid in the brush, carefully avoiding parties of searchers. The next morning they headed for Dodge City, four hundred miles away, on "borrowed" horses.

The couple registered at Deacon Cox's Boarding House in Dodge City as Dr. and Mrs. J. H. Holliday. Doc felt he owed Kate a great deal for rescuing him from the "hanging tree" in Fort Griffin. He was determined to do anything in his power to make her happy.

Kate gave up being a prostitute and inhabiting the saloons. Doc gave up gambling and hung out his dentist's shingle again. All of Doc's good intentions were totally unappreciated and did not endure for long.

Kate stood the quiet and boredom of respectable living as long as she could. Then she told Doc that she was going back to the bright lights and excitement of the dance halls and gambling dens.

Consequently, the two split up, as they were destined to do many times during the remainder of Doc's life.

In late August, 1879 Doc got into an argument with a local gunman, named Mike Gordon. The two took the argument to the street where Doc invited Gordon to start shooting whenever he felt like it. Gordon accepted the invitation and wound up dead with three shots in his belly.

Again, a lynch mob formed with plans to lynch Holliday. Before they reached him, Doc headed back to Dodge City where he hoped to join his friend Wyatt Earp.

He arrived only to find that Wyatt had gone to a new silver strike, in a place called Tombstone, Arizona. Doc headed for Tombstone. Unknown to Doc, Big Nose Kate was also enroute to Tombstone.

The two ran into each other in Prescott, Arizona where Doc was winning heavily at the tables and pocketed $40,000 in winnings. Kate was happy to keep him company. Finally, Kate went on to Tombstone, where, in 1880, she was running a sporting house. Doc stayed in Prescott with his hot card game.

Finally, with his winnings in his pocket, he followed Kate to Tombstone.

On March 15, 1881, four masked men held up a stagecoach near Contention, Arizona and in the attempt, killed the stage driver. Holliday was accused of being one of the holdup men.

The sheriff, who was investigating the hold-up, found Kate on one of her drunken binges, still berating Doc for throwing her out. Feeding her yet even more whiskey, the sheriff persuaded her to sign an affidavit that Doc had been one of the masked highwaymen and had killed the stage driver.

When she sobered up, she recanted her statement and Doc was released. This, however, ended her relationship with Holliday.

Kate kept trying to renew the friendship. She made a trip to Glenwood Springs, Colorado where Holliday was near death from tuberculosis. It was the last time she saw him.

After Holliday died, Kate married George Cummings, a Colorado blacksmith. The marriage lasted only a year. Too old to work at her old trade, Kate took a job with John Howard as a housekeeper in Dos Cabezas, Arizona, where she worked until his death in 1930.

Kate applied to the Arizona Pioneers Home and was finally accepted after a six-month wait. She passed away a week before her ninetieth birthday.

She was buried at the Pioneer Cemetery in Prescott, Arizona. Her headstone simply reads Mary K. Cummings.

Chapter 4

Ah Toy

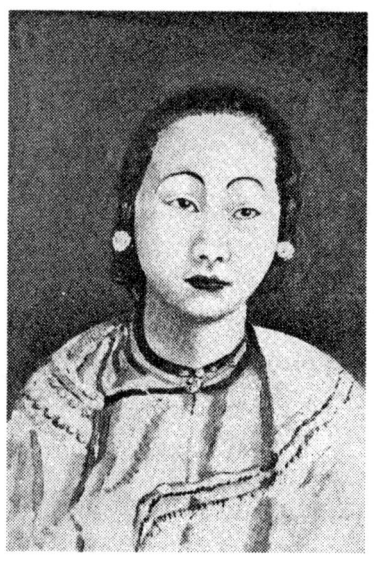

Ah Toy
(Mercaldo Archives)

Chinese slave girls were bought for little more than pennies in China and then brought to California for sale to the highest bidder. Even the Mann Act, enacted in 1910 prohibiting the interstate transportation of women for immoral purposes, didn't help them.

Donaldina Cameron, director of the Presbyterian Mission in San Francisco, said, "All of the slave girls in San Francisco, particularly those who occupied the cribs, were shamefully mistreated by their masters. They received no part of their earnings, and most of them never left their dens except for brief periods."

The Chinese girl was considered of little value in her own country. It was, most times, her parents that sold her into slavery in the first place.

Ah Toy was one Chinese girl that rose above her brethren. She sailed to California with her husband in 1849 aboard a China Clipper ship. A few weeks out to sea, Ah Toy's husband died. Ah Toy soon became the Captain's mistress.

When Ah Toy landed in San Francisco, she carried a considerable amount of gold, lavished on her by the generous captain.

Donaldina Cameron
(The Cameron House)

Ah Toy was attractive. As she strolled down the Embarcadero she could hardly help notice the attention given her by a group of male followers. Unlike China, where a woman was considered worthless, women as ravishing as Ah Toy drove the men wild in San Francisco.

"If men became this aroused over the glimpse of a Chinese woman, surely they would pay for the privilege of a closer look," she told herself. Even though Ah Toy had shared her favors with the Captain, she was not a prostitute at this time.

Ah Toy rented a two-room building and added a platform in one room. Small peep holes were drilled into a wall. She decided to open a "look but don't touch show". Her show was a great success.

She hired a big Chinese man to collect one ounce of gold from each man occupying a peep hole. When each peep hole was occupied, Ah Toy would appear on the small stage, wearing a form-fitting silk kimono. Underneath, she was totally nude.

Her show lasted only a few moments. But as she seductively removed her kimono, the lusty miners at the peep holes stamped their feet and howled at the sight of the beautiful Chinese girl.

Ah Toy later encountered a problem with her gold collection process. Her Chinese collector could not distinguish the difference in a gold nugget and a brass nugget. Some miners were paying her with fake nuggets.

She tried to sue the men, but her case was dismissed. Ah Toy then stopped her peep show and turned to a more lucrative practice. She began selling sex to high-placed businessmen.

She opened a chain of brothels, importing her own girls from China, many as young as 11. Most thought they were coming to California to marry a wealthy husband.

The new arrivals were herded into an immense underground cavern known as the "Queen's Room".

Donaldina Cameron and three Chinese girls she rescued.
(San Francisco Library)

Here, older Chinese women took over. These women had been prostitutes themselves and knew the ways to please a man. They taught the new girls how to please their men, and more important, how to entice them into cubicles.

When the girls were rested, buyers were notified of the auction to take place.

Ah Toy became quite wealthy and eventually went back to China to live in comfort. Most other

Chinese girls simply continued suffering at the hands of the crib owners.

Donaldina Cameron had come to the Presbyterian Mission Home in San Francisco in 1895 to teach sewing to Asian girls and women.

Most of these women were brought to California as slaves. Some were only six years of age when the mission rescued them.

Most often they were kidnapped, but just as frequently, they were sold by their parents in China, and forced to work as domestics and prostitutes in the United States. Shortly after Donaldina arrived, her supervisor died. This threw Donaldina into the position of director.

She is credited with saving more than three thousand women and children during her forty-seven years at the mission. To those she rescued, she was known as *"White Angel"* and as *"Lo Mo"*, which means Beloved Mother.

Slave dealers and brothel owners did not hold her in such esteem. To them she was *"White Devil"*.

The rescues usually consisted only of Donaldina and a companion. They would simply walk past the Chinese guards and escort the girls back to the mission. The guards were usually so confused and surprised at the sight of a white woman in the Chinese ghetto that they turned and ran.

Once safely back in the mission, Donaldina and other missionaries helped give the girls a better life. They were taught English—and perhaps reading and writing—according to their situations. The girls were introduced to Christianity and the Bible, as well as cooking, cleaning and sewing.

Chinese cribs in squalid condition in San Francisco. (San Francisco Library)

Many of these women were smuggled into the United States, circumventing immigration laws that excluded them. They were simply commodities that were bought and sold as property. The system was known as the *"yellow slave trade."*

Bogus contracts were created to keep the system working. The contracts were written with insurmountable conditions, making it impossible for the women to purchase their own freedom. Some say the number of Asian women who died in enslaved conditions in San Francisco numbered in the thousands.

Gaining entry into the United States was complicated for the Chinese because of the Chinese Exclusion Acts of 1882, 1888, 1892, and 1902 and the Immigration Act of 1924.

These acts increased restrictions on Asian immigrants, especially laborers. Only students, teachers or merchants were admitted to America. The acts were clearly discriminatory, as no other national group was denied entry to the country.

According to Paul Q. Chow, who wrote a thesis on the subject, the fear was that laborers from China would take jobs away from European-American workers. This fear was made worse because of the severe economic depression facing the country at that time.

When Donaldina Cameron arrived in San Francisco from the San Joaquin Valley, her intention was to devote a "single year" working in the Chinese Presbyterian Mission at 920 Sacramento Street.

When she became aware of the slavery and conditions in Chinatown, she felt repulsed. From a mild-mannered missionary girl, Donaldina was transformed into a zealous social reformer. She became fanatically committed to wiping out the horrors of yellow slavery.

A *San Francisco Examiner* article by Michael Svanevik and Shirley Burgett detailed the lengths to which Cameron would go.

Chinese temple in San Francisco.
(Google Images)

"Slavery, was a fact of life in China," they wrote. "For centuries, young girls were taught to think of themselves as creatures almost purely for the enjoyment of men and were sold as merchandize to be wives, concubines or prostitutes."

Most of those arriving in California during the gold rush were sold for immoral purposes. State officials were bought off by the Chinese slavers and refused to recognize the existence of the slavery practice.

The majority of the girls in San Francisco's Chinatown worked in cribs—narrow cells that accommodated two to six girls. They were required to service all comers, most of whom were white.

Patrons paid twenty-five to fifty-cents for sexual services. Young boys were admitted for fifteen-cents.

According to the *San Francisco Examiner*, The Presbyterian Mission spearheaded reform against the yellow slave trade as early as the 1870s. Margaret Culbertson, then the mission's director, instituted raids to liberate captive children.

Cameron became the scourge of the underworld, the *Examiner* wrote. "She came to know every back alley and rooftop in Chinatown. She undertook rescues of young captives who requested assistance or when maltreatment of a child was reported."

When denied access to a crib or parlor, she relied on an unofficial alliance she had developed with San Francisco Police Sergeant Jack Manion, commander of the so-called Chinatown Squad. Manion sympathized with Cameron and ordered his men to "give her whatever she wants."

Police officers in plain clothes gained entry where Cameron could not. They simply pounded down doors with sledgehammers, crowbars and axes.

Plans for such raids were generally kept very secret, but word of them sometimes leaked out and the girls were herded into passageways, tunnels or secret rooms.

The *San Francisco Examiner* noted that Cameron did not limit her activities to San Francisco. She led raids in virtually every city on the Pacific Coast. She admitted that she often found it necessary to "break the letter though not the spirit of the law."

Not all girls came to the mission willingly. Many became so frightened at the appearance of Cameron that they jeopardized their own rescues, the Examiner report said. At least some were forced into the mission against their will.

"The activities of Cameron and the Presbyterians endangered a very lucrative operation," the Examiner reporters explained. "Slave girls represented big money both for the brokers who imported them and for corrupt officials who looked the other way."

During the 1850s, girls sold for between one-hundred and five-hundred-dollars. By the end of World War I, prices had risen to as high as seven-thousand-dollars. Yellow slavery flourished until the 1930s.

The slavery overlords expressed their displeasure with Cameron's crusade. On one occasion, a dynamite bomb was found on the steps of 920 Sacramento Street and disarmed without any damage.

The mission also opened its doors to girls such as Tye Leung, who was born in the United States. Tye lived in a two-room apartment in Chinatown with her mother, father, six brothers and one sister.

Tye's parents had arrived before the Chinese Exclusion Acts were enacted. Tye's parents had allowed her and her brothers and a sister to adapt to American ways. The girls even attended school.

Yet, the father and mother clung to some of their Chinese culture. They selected a bridegroom for their daughter. Tye firmly rejected the idea that she would marry the man her parents had chosen for her.

He was a complete stranger to her and wanted to cart her off to Butte, Montana, a place she knew absolutely nothing about.

Rather than go through with such a marriage, Tye secretly left the home of her mother and father and sought asylum in Donaldina Cameron's mission.

Donaldina Cameron retired in 1938 after forty-seven years with the mission. Four years later, the mission was renamed the Cameron House in her honor. Donaldina Cameron died in 1968 at the age of ninety-eight.

Chapter 5

The Girls of Cripple Creek

The cabin of Bob Womack, discoverer of Cripple Creek. (Cripple Creek History)

Blanche Barton was the first prostitute to arrive at Cripple Creek, Colorado. She was encouraged by Bob Womack, the discoverer of Cripple Creek, to set up her striped tent in Poverty Gulch, just down the hill from his cabin.

While she was the first of her trade to arrive, Blanche had plenty of business opportunities. Among her customers was Tim Hussey, an energetic miner that was always short of cash.

Instead of paying Blanche in cash or gold dust, Hussey would assign one-eighth interest in mining claims as payment. Blanche had trouble understanding the claims and took them to Bob Womack to decipher.

Cripple Creek became a boom town.
(Google Images)

Bob explained to her that she now owned twenty-seven one-eighth interests, all in the same claim. She became one of Cripple Creek's most successful entrepreneurs.

As more and more ladies arrived to take part in the Cripple Creek boom, men could not walk down the streets to do business in town without being propositioned. Cripple Creek wives suffered as well. They had little desire to do their daily shopping in the presence of the prostitutes.

This caused two things to happen. All the dance halls and their girl employees were moved to Myers Avenue, where they would be free from harassment as long as they paid their head tax, went to church on Sunday and behaved in public.

Myers Avenue thus became heavily populated with parlor houses, brothels and cribs. The most famous was Pearl DeVere's Old Homestead. It was also the most expensive

Pearl DeVere's Old Homestead parlor house.
(Google Images)

Pearl came to Cripple Creek at age thirty-one, red-haired and beautiful. Her family was completely unaware of Pearl's chosen avocation. They believed Pearl was a dress designer.

She was intensely popular, and married mill owner C.B. Flynn. In April 1896, fire blazed through much of the town of Cripple Creek, wiping out both Pearl's parlor house as well as Flynn's mill.

Both Flynn and Pearl were bankrupt from the destructive fire. Flynn took a job smelting iron in Monterrey, Mexico to get his finances back in order. Pearl stayed in Cripple Creek where she rebuilt her parlor house.

She named it "The Old Homestead." It had all the elegant amenities of the wealthy, including electricity, running water and two bathtubs.

It was an instant hit when it opened in 1896. Pearl employed four beautiful girls to staff the new

49

parlor house. Each girl had her own room, complete with a handsome dresser, fancy changing screen, and storage trunk.

Pearl's parlor house offered a feature that was really special for the miners. It was a viewing room, where they could see Pearl's beauties sans clothing while making a choice of which one they wanted to entertain them.

Only the wealthy could afford Pearl's place. The price for a night at the Old Homestead was two-hundred-fifty dollars. Gold miners were making three-dollars a day. Any new gentleman appearing at Pearl's needed a letter of recommendation.

One night, Pearl hosted a lavish party. Not feeling well, herself, she went upstairs and took some morphine to help her sleep. This was a common practice at the time.

She asked one of her girls to stay with her while she slept. The girl, however, fell asleep. When the girl awoke, Pearl's breathing was labored and she girl sent for a doctor. It was too late, as Pearl had overdosed.

Pearl's relatives were notified of her death. Her sister traveled to Cripple Creek to escort her body back home to Indiana. The sister was horrified when she learned Pearl's true vocation. She headed home, leaving Pearl's body where it lay.

Most people around Cripple Creek thought Pearl was wealthy. It was found that instead of being wealthy, her estate did not contain enough money to bury her properly.

Plans were made to auction off Pearl's elegant French gown. Before that could be done, however, a letter with a Denver postmark arrived at Fraley Bros. and Lampman funeral parlor. It contained one-thousand-dollars and a note stipulating the money was not only for Pearl's burial expenses, but that she was to be buried in her beloved French gown.

Today, The Old Homestead is a museum, including many pieces of its original furniture.

Chapter 6

The San Francisco Girls

Women were so few in number in San Francisco in 1848 that word of one passing by in the street would quickly empty a saloon of its inhabitants. Some estimates put the number of females arriving in San Francisco during 1848 at less than 100. Some of the ships from Chile and Peru arrived in San Francisco carrying women that were often not wives, widows, nor maids.

Sally Stanford
(California State Library)

Most of the men and families came overland, while those women intending to engage in prostitution came by ship, from Mazatlan, Guaymas, or San

53

Blas. Few, if any, had money for passage. Spanish-Californian Captain Jose Fernandez explained, "They did not pay passage on the ships. When they reached San Francisco, the captains sold them to the highest bidder."

When any ship arrived from a Mexican port, there were men who took two or three small boats or a launch out to meet the ship. The men boarded the ship and paid the passages for ten to twelve of the women.

The women were taken immediately to cantinas, where the newcomers were forced to prostitute themselves for half a year, during which the proprietors took the bulk of their earnings.

Little was written about these so-called women of the night, but Curt Gentry did tackle the subject in his 1964 book, "The Madams of San Francisco."

According to Gentry, "Almost all of those arriving were of Mexican, Spanish, or French descent. Most came from Mexico, Central, and South America. From early 1849 through at least 1852, these areas were to provide more of California's prostitutes (and dance-hall girls) than all other countries combined."

One writer, William S. McCollum, in his book, "California As I saw It", carried a dim view of the women prostitutes as a whole. "The Senoritas are not fascinating, because they are not pretty—they are very willing to be gazed at, however, and are inclined to coquetry. I must confess I prefer something lighter—and less greasy—more graceful and less indolent, and above all, something which can speak English."

This was an 1890 poster showing two whores and their madam.
(Fille De Joie Erotica Festival)

Mark Twain wrote the following about the Nicaraguan women that landed in San Francisco, "They are virtuous, according to their lights, but I guess that their lights are a little dim."

One author painted an even more distasteful picture of the women from Paraguay. "Everybody smokes in Paraguay, and nearly every female above thirteen years of age chews. Only imagine yourself about to kiss a magnificent little Hebe, arrayed in satin and flashing with diamonds; she puts you back with one delicate hand, while with the fair, tapered fingers of the other she draws forth from her mouth a brownish-black roll of tobacco, quite two inches long and looking like a monstrous grub, and deposits the delicate morsel on the rim of your sombrero, puts up her face and is ready for a salute!"

In that period, with so few females in California, wrote one Sacramento woman, "Every man thought every woman in that day a beauty. Even I have had men come forty miles over the mountains, just to look at me, and I never was called a handsome woman in my best day even by my most ardent admirers."

No California madam was quite as famous as Sally Stanford who maintained perhaps the classiest house in San Francisco during the 1930s. Her house became so famous a landmark that it was included on the city's sightseeing tours.

Sally Stanford was born Mabel Janice Busby. She changed her name while walking down Kearney Street one day and saw a newspaper headline, "Stanford Wins Big Game".

"That's for me!" she told herself. "I'm going after big game."

A story is told about a young policeman, bursting into her establishment and announcing, "I'm bustin' this place!"

"Before you do that buster," Sally coolly told him, "I suggest you go out to the kitchen and talk to your dad—we were just having a cup of coffee."

New York's famous madam, Polly Adler, once visited Sally. Adler told Sally, "You know the madam's lament—everybody goes upstairs but us."

After police closed her down in 1949, Sally opened the Valhalla restaurant in Sausalito. She later was elected to the City Council and served as mayor of the town.

There were some that claimed the Chinese prostitutes in San Francisco were responsible for the high rate of syphilis that kept the hospitals filled.

Historian Charles Caldwell Dobie found this accusation could not be true, inasmuch as by the end of 1851, the total of Chinese women in the city numbered only about seven. The number of prostitutes from other races plying their trade in San Francisco at the same time was well over one thousand.

Gold miners seemed to have a particular fascination with the French women arriving in San Francisco with the obvious intention of setting up a red-light shop.

Albert Benard, a thirty-one year old Frenchman who came to San Francisco, worked as an actor and later as a journalist for the city's first French newspaper.

His view of the French women who came to San Francisco was certainly different than that of the gold miners casting admiring glances.

"If the poor fellows had known what these women had been in Paris, where one could pick them up on the boulevards and have them for almost nothing, they might not have been as free with their offers of $500 or $600 a night," Benard wrote.

Some of the women, he said, made enough in one month in San Francisco to go home to France and live on their incomes, but many were not so lucky. "No doubt, they were blind to their own wrinkled and faded skins, and were too confident in their ability to deceive Americans regarding the dates on their birth certificates."

The French women did not first go to work in the brothels. Instead, they rented their own apartments. Then, from noon until midnight, they hired themselves out to gambling establishments at large salaries.

Their jobs in the establishments were simply to grace the gambling tables, giving the gamblers a little something extra to look at. After they finished work, they were able to entertain callers in their small apartments. They undoubtedly began filling their evening appointment books while still at the tables.

In their native land most of the French girls were "streetwalkers of the cheapest sort." Whatever their background, these women knew how to pleasure the women-hungry gold miners.

A miner, whether he wanted it or not, would be given a bath, a shave, and new clothes to put on before enjoying the services of the French demimondes.

The miners were grateful and willing to pay for such pleasures, however brief. It was a welcome break from the backbreaking, and too often, unrewarding work in the gold diggings.

Another story is told by writer Michelle Jolly about the time that Charles Cora accompanied his mistress, Arabella Ryan, to the theatre in San Francisco.

During the play, the gentlemen seated in front of the couple rose and demanded that Cora and Arabella leave the theater. Arabella, commonly known as Belle, was a prostitute, and the gentleman requesting that she leave was U.S. Marshal William Richardson. The marshal felt Belle's presence offended his wife.

Hanging of Charles Cora and William Casey.
(Bancroft Library)

Charles Cora refused to leave. Two days later, Richardson and Cora met and exchanged words over the incident. Cora pulled a pistol and shot Richardson to death.

The "Cora Case", was a favorite subject of the city's newest newspaper, *The Daily Evening Bulletin*. In an effort to boost circulation of his newcomer newspaper, the publisher chose "reform" as his readership vehicle.

The publisher, James King of William, a name he used to differentiate himself from other James Kings, made the Cora Case a symbol of San Francisco's problems.

King charged that San Francisco's most successful prostitutes, such as Belle, the mistress of Charles Cora, worked hand-in-glove with gamblers and power-seeking politicians to dominate and corrupt city politics.

When Charles Cora's trial resulted in a hung jury, King's *Daily Evening Bulletin* trumpeted,

"'Hung be the heavens with black!' The money of the gambler and the prostitutes has succeeded, and Cora has another respite!"

King was shot after publishing a muck-raking article against county supervisor William Casey, who was also a local newspaperman. The shooting of King caused an outrage and a citizens Vigilance Committee was formed.

The vigilante's first act was to raid the jail, taking both William Casey and Charles Cora. After a brief trial by the committee Casey and Cora were sentenced to be hanged.

Minutes before the hanging, Belle married Charles Cora in his cell inside Vigilante headquarters.

In the meantime, a different culture of prostitution was developing in San Francisco during the second half of 1849. During that time, a wave of European and white American prostitutes arrived in the area and took advantage of the chances for social mobility in the sexually permissive city.

Observer Caleb T. Fay wrote, "The only aristocracy we had here at the time were the gamblers and prostitutes." Other observers said prostitutes were part of the upper echelons of San Francisco society.

Not only were they the most elegantly dressed women in San Francisco . . . both on the street and in the gambling saloons where they worked, but they actually set the style for the ladies in the city.

Furthermore, their social circles involved the most prominent men in town.

Chapter 7

The Santa Cruz Girls

Santa Cruz County, California officials took a dim view of prostitution early on. The first known arrest for keeping a house of ill-fame took place in Watsonville, in 1860.

Nuanor Samilla and Filleppe Escalante were jailed. Each were charged with a misdemeanor, found guilty, and given a fine of fifteen-dollars.

The next attempt at curbing the ill-famed houses in Santa Cruz came in 1868. Two men, by the names of Malson and Shaw, were tried on a charge of keeping a *bawdy-house*. They were released when the jury failed to agree on a verdict.

Most parlor house girls were well-dressed.
(The Police Gazette)

Like many western towns, the only effort to curb prostitution more often came from the annual grand jury. In Santa Cruz County, it became a time honored ritual for the grand jury to probe the town's houses of ill-repute after they had looked at conditions at the poor farm and the jail.

Writer Phil Read, in an article titled "Harlots and Whorehouses," noted that the grand juries of 1872 and 1877 showed more determination than usual in shutting down the brothels.

They adopted the motto "Let the Augean Stables be cleansed," showing a flair for classical literature in its reference to Hercules cleaning thirty years of refuse from the stables of Augeas in one day.

The 1872 Santa Cruz County grand jury indicted sixteen people, including the three most famous Santa Cruz madams. These were Emma Cooper, Maria McDermott and Madame Pauline.

Not all prostitutes were degraded and down-trodden. Madame Pauline was a good example. She was a familiar figure on the streets of Santa Cruz for thirty years. She owned three brothels in the county and was known to do good deeds throughout those years.

Even the normally chaste *Santa Cruz Sentinel* eulogized Madame Pauline in this way: "In a quiet way, she did many charitable acts. No poor person ever came away from her empty handed. More than one poor family she assisted, and the world was none the wiser."

When the 1877 grand jury attempted to close down all of the houses of prostitution, a group of prominent citizens, including a number of women, sent a petition to the District Attorney, asking him to defer prosecuting Madame Pauline. Their petition read,

> "...she was a liberal and spirited citizen, contributing generously to charitable and public projects...and that she had given something to bring the Santa Cruz Railroad into our town..."

Sheriff Bob Orton raided the Front Street brothels in 1877. To his chagrin, a newspaper article on May 12, 1877, supported Madame Pauline.

> "Pauline, proprietress of a house of prostitution, has kept a very orderly and quiet house. This house was completely unobjectionable to even the nearest neighbors."

Madame Pauline was born Florinni De Paulinni in 1847 at New York City. She was married twice. Her first husband was George Prince and her second was Jim Ogden. Both ended in divorce and left her with three children to support.

She arrived in Watsonville, California in 1867, and began work in a brothel on Pajaro Street. By 1871, Pauline had saved enough money to buy the house where she worked.

She later invested in other real estate in the downtown area of Watsonville. The following year, she moved her brothel operation to Santa Cruz while retaining her interests in Watsonville.

Her children did well. Ironically, perhaps, her daughter, Edna Ogden, entered a convent in San Bernardino and rose to the position of Mother Superior of her order.

Madame Pauline always remained close to her family, including her oldest son, Pearly Prince, a land agent for the Southern Pacific Railroad in the Los Angeles area, and a second son, who was in real estate in San Francisco.

When underage boys walked timidly into her parlor, Pauline good-naturedly escorted them down the back stairs and out the door.

In 1885, her neighbor Dr. Benjamin Knight approached Pauline. He told her about a patient of his that was about to give birth. He described her house as in a state of complete disarray. The pregnant woman lay on a pile of blankets in the middle of the floor in critical condition.

The only furnishings in the house were two chairs, a rickety bench, and one worn-out table upon which rested three potatoes, the only food the family had.

What touched the doctor even more were the faces of the six children standing silently about the room, all in need of clothes. The eldest girl wore a dress fashioned from an old grain sack.

Dr. Knight had willingly donated his medical services, but he feared for the plight of the children.

The following day, Madame Pauline hired a buggy, rode out to the house of the family, and brought them all back to town. She moved them into a frame house she owned on Water Street, and put the father to work doing maintenance on her various properties.

Madame Pauline died of apoplexy at her home in 1898 at the age of fifty-one. Her estate was valued at more than forty-thousand-dollars.

When the Santa Cruz County grand jury began its annual crusade again in 1877, it might have wished it hadn't stirred up the wrath of feisty Jane Allison. She mounted a formidable challenge to the local system of jurisprudence. When Lady Jane was done, she left half the male population in town blushing.

When Jane was called before the court on a charge of prostitution and disorderly conduct, she vowed to fight the charge, even "if it took all summer."

To represent her, Jane hired lawyer Joseph Skirm, a determined representative of underdogs. He was also considered the most brilliant barrister in Santa Cruz County.

When Judge Albert Hagan called the court to order, Jane and her attorney sat quietly as the jury was impaneled and Attorney John Logan presented the people's case.

Attorney Skirm then approached the bench and informed the judge he had a list of witnesses he wanted subpoenaed.

When the judge asked for the list, Jane stood up, took out her little black book, and read a total of one-hundred-forty names, including most of the male residents of Santa Cruz.

Attorney Skirm had a field day with his cross-examination of the witnesses. Most sat intimidated with Jane's presence in the courtroom.

When all the arguments were heard, the jury retired for deliberations. The jury rapped on the jury-room door, saying they had not been able to agree.

The court refused to let them out, keeping them locked up for another two hours. Judge Hagan, Attorney Skirm and Jane Allison all adjourned to a nearby restaurant for a leisurely supper.

Judge Hagan then called the jury back into the court. They were still unable to agree. The judge called a mistrial and sent the panel home.

Jane Allison returned to work at Emma Cooper's whorehouse.

Chapter 8

Calamity   Jane

Here are pictures of Calamity Jane in her typical men's army uniform and in some rather feminine garb she seldom wore.   (Wyoming State Museum)

Some writers have depicted Martha Jane "Calamity Jane" Cannary as being a frontier prostitute among all her other strenuous activities.

One rumor alleges she had an affair with Duncan Blackburn, a stagecoach robber in Deadwood, Dakota Territory, and bore him a son.

Another reference, is in *The Encyclopedia of Western Lawmen and Outlaws*, that says

"...(Calamity) was often a mistress to lawmen and gunmen, and, periodically, a common prostitute in western towns such as Deadwood, S.D."

She was crude and manly, which might have been out of necessity. Her job as an army scout with such notables as General George Custer, required her to associate with men.

In her own short autobiography, Calamity wrote:

> "Up to this time, I had always worn the costume of my sex. When I joined Custer, I donned the uniform of a soldier. It was a bit awkward at first, but I soon got to be perfectly at home in men's clothes."

Biographer Roberta Sollid says that while driving in a wagon train, her sex may have been detected. This occurred when the wagon-master noted she did not cuss her mules with the enthusiasm expected from a graduate of Patrick and Saulsbury's Black Hills Stage Line, as she had represented herself to be.

There are several stories about how she got the nickname of "Calamity". One version is the one she herself wrote in her autobiography:

> "It was on Goose Creek, Wyoming, where the town of Sheridan is now located. Captain Egan was in command of the post. We were ordered out to quell an uprising of the Indians, and were out for several days, had

numerous skirmishes during which six of the soldiers were killed and several severely wounded.

"When fired upon, Captain Egan was shot. I was riding in advance and, on hearing the firing, turned in my saddle and saw the Captain reeling in his saddle as though about to fall.

"I turned my horse and galloped back with all haste to his side and got there in time to catch him as he was falling. I lifted him onto my horse in front of me and succeeded in getting him safely to the Fort.

"Captain Egan, on recovering, laughingly said: 'I name you Calamity Jane, the heroine of the plains.' I have borne that name up to the present time."

There are other accounts of how she was pinned with the nickname of "Calamity". One, from an old-timer, who said, "If she sat on a fence rail, it would rare up and buck her off."

The *St. Paul Dispatch* wrote: "She got her name from a faculty she has had of producing a ruction at any time and place on short notice."

In 1876, *The Black Hills Pioneer* in Deadwood, South Dakota, headlined: "Calamity Jane Has Arrived". Calamity, herself explains:

"During the month of June, I acted as a pony express rider carrying the

U.S. mail between Deadwood and Custer, a distance of fifty miles, over one of the roughest trails in the Black Hills country.

"Many of the riders before me had been held up and robbed of their packages, mail and money they carried, for that was the only means of getting mail and money between those points.

"It was considered the most dangerous route in the Hills, but as my reputation as a rider and quick shot was well known, I was molested very little, for the toll gathers looked on me as being a good fellow, and they knew that I never missed my mark.

"I made the round trip every two days which was considered good riding in that country. I remained around Deadwood all that summer visiting all the camps within an area of one-hundred-miles. My friend, Wild Bill, remained in Deadwood during the summer with the exception of occasional visits to the camps."

Some writers have tried to connect Wild Bill Hickok and Calamity Jane romantically, but the evidence is thin. Hickok, himself, wrote the following:

"I do not know much about her early life. I guess nobody else does but herself. Her maiden name was Martha Canary, and she was born in Princeton, Mo., in 1852.

Wild Bill Hickok
(Google Images)

"She had friends and very positive opinions of the things that a girl could enjoy, and she soon gained a local reputation for horsemanship and skill as a rifle shot.

"Before she was twenty General Cook appointed her as a scout under me. From that time on her life was pretty lively all the time. She had unlimited nerve and entered into the work with enthusiasm, doing good service on a number of occasions.

"Though she did not do a man's share of the heavy work, she has gone in places where old frontiersmen were unwilling to trust themselves, and her courage and good-fellowship made her popular with every man in the command."

It is from her biography, published in "Women in History" on the Internet, that an inference between Calamity and prostitution is assumed. The biographer wrote:

"In 1881, Jane went to Wyoming; returning to Miles City in 1882 and starting a ranch on "the Yellow Stone" raising stock and cattle. She also kept "a way-side inn, where the weary traveler could be accommodated with food, drink, or trouble if he looked for it."

She left that in 1883, traveling west and reaching Ogden, California, in late 1883, then San Francisco in 1884. That summer, she left for Texas, and reached El Paso in the fall."

In her own biography, Calamity writes about her marriage.

"While in El Paso, I met Mr. Clinton Burk, a native of Texas, who I married in August 1885 (at 33 years old). As I thought I had traveled through life long enough alone and thought it was about time to take a partner for the rest of my days.

"We remained in Texas leading a quiet home life until 1889. On October 28th, 1887, I became the mother of a baby girl, the very image of her father, at least that's what he said, but who has the temper of its mother."

Calamity did not write of other men, or children. There is some evidence that she was involved with a Robert Dorsett in the 1880s. A court record from November 1888 states that "Charles Townley, an unmarried man, and Jane Doe (alias Calamity Jane), an unmarried woman, (did at some time) unlawfully bed, cohabit and live together...without being then and there married."

From the same document, Calamity had relationships with a Wyoming rancher named King and a William Steers. Nothing indicates that she was anything more than a promiscuous woman during those years.

Calamity doesn't write anywhere about her baby girl, or her name, even in her memoirs.

According to Nash, in his Encyclopedia of Western Lawmen and Outlaws, "Very little of the vast amount of literature produced about this frontier character is factually reliable."

Chapter 9

Mary Ellen Pleasant

At birth, Mary Ellen "Mammy" Pleasant had no last name. She said she was the illegitimate child of a Virginia governor's son (John H. Pleasants) and an enslaved Haitian Voodoo priestess. (As used in this context, the word "Voodoo" means spirit, and refers to the religion descended from a number of African cultures.)

While she won many of her frequent battles

Mary Ellen Pleasant

against inequities for others, Mary Ellen was never quite able to win the battle for her own good name.

Mary Ellen was born a slave near Augusta, Georgia between 1814 and 1817. According to ships records and confirming testimony, Mary Ellen arrived in

75

San Francisco in 1852 to escape persecution under the Fugitive Slave Law of 1850.

As a child, she was sent to work in the service of a merchant in Nantucket, Massachusetts. She was a precocious child, and according to her final memoir, could recall the entire day's transactions in the general store where she clerked. This was indeed a feat, in that Mary Ellen could barely read and write.

When her indenture ended in 1841, Mary Ellen married James W. Smith, a wealthy mulatto. While both Mary Ellen and her husband were mulattos, they each could pass as white.

Mary Ellen and her husband became allied with the Underground Railroad, helping slaves escape to freedom by various routes, but mainly on the railroad from Nova Scotia to Virginia (near Harper's Ferry).

James died suddenly. There were some who felt his death came at Mary Ellen's hand. Nevertheless, he left Mary Ellen a wealthy woman.

Pleasant continued her rescue work for the slaves by sneaking onto plantations and soon became a much-hunted rescue worker. She fled to New Orleans to hide out with the family of her second husband.

In New Orleans, Mary Ellen had the opportunity to study with social-activist Voodoo Queen Mam'zelle, Marie LaVeaux. LaVeaux had invented a way to use Voodoo to aid the disenfranchised, and Mary Ellen wanted to learn it.

The strategy she learned was how to use the secrets of the rich to get aid for the poor, a "model" that would serve her well in San Francisco.

Slave owners hated Mary Ellen and continued on her trail. She was forced to head west. She arrived in San Francisco April 7, 1852. The population at the time was about forty-thousand people and to serve them there were seven hundred gambling establishments.

It was not a safe place, with five murders occurring every six days.

The California Fugitive Slave Act stipulated that anyone without freedom papers could be captured and returned to slavery. Mary Ellen took two identities to conceal the fact that she had no papers.

As Mrs. Ellen Smith, she worked as a white boardinghouse steward-cook. As Mrs. Pleasants, she continued her work as a black woman to help her people escape from slavery.

Working as Mrs. Smith, she was able to get jobs and privileges for "colored" people in San Francisco. She gained the nickname, "The Black City Hall." As Mrs. Pleasants, she used her money to help ex-slaves fight unfair laws and to get lawyers or set up a business in California.

Mary Ellen became an expert capitalist. Her own assets grew and she prospered. But when European emigrants began taking the menial jobs, anti-black sentiment and national depression mounted.

She traveled east again to help John Brown end slavery. Their plans involved dangerous ventures.

Mary Ellen wrote, "I'd rather be a corpse than a coward."

John Brown was hanged for his efforts, and Mary Ellen narrowly escaped. Back in California, she continued to fight. When the Emancipation Proclamation and the California Right-of-Testimony of 1863, were passed, Mary Ellen openly declared her race as being black, not white.

She orchestrated court battles to challenge the right of testimony, and in 1868, her battle for the right to ride the San Francisco trolleys set a precedent in the California Supreme Court.

Mary Ellen is said to have amassed a fortune of thirty million.

When Montgomery Street auctioneers put Lola Montez' jewels up for sale, Mammy Pleasant was the principal purchaser.

In San Francisco, the Barbary Coast was confined to Pacific Street. Never-the-less, the price of properties several blocks away declined because of their proximity to the Pacific Street brothels.

The ambitious Mammy Pleasant bought a number of these depressed properties, sure that as growth in the city occurred, so would the value of the property.

She was right. Anything on Montgomery and Kearney Streets between Washington and Broadway, appreciated many fold.

Mary Ellen, without appearing on the scene personally, moved a madam and her girls out of one ramshackle house on Kearney Street, rebuilt it, and spent fifteen-thousand-dollars re-furnishing it as a luxurious parlor house.

As far as the public knew, the parlor house was owned by the madam who leased it from Mammy Pleasant, a "Madam Em" or "French Em".

Some claimed Mary Ellen stopped at nothing in her unrelenting drive for wealth and power. Harry Sinclair Drago, author of *Notorious Ladies of the Frontier,* said, "At least on four occasions, she took girls out of the houses of prostitution, transformed them into young ladies with a veneer of culture, and married them off to rich men."

Her next step was to blackmail these young women by threatening to expose their past.

If a man refused to marry one of her protégés after having sex with them, Mammy Pleasant had her servant produce a baby, bought or stolen, and confront the alleged father and bring him to terms.

Chapter 10

Storyville Girls

Just south of the old Basin Street train station in New Orleans (which is now gone), lay the French Quarter. Here, too, was "Storyville", the nation's first legally designated prostitution district.

It was a fast-growing part of New Orleans during its twenty-year lifetime. More and more prostitutes, jazz bands and saloons crowded the Storyville area, adding to the city's reputation as the "Babylon of the South".

Storyville was, ironically, created to curb the very wanton ways that pervaded the district. City reformers hoped to regulate and limit prostitution in its fair city by confining it to a designated area.

To do so, they turned a "not very nice" residential area into the only district in which prostitutes could live and work. This, they hoped, would keep the brothels from trashing other neighborhoods and lowering property values.

Intentional or not, city officials created a nationally known center of vice. It's assumed that City Councilman Sidney Story, who sponsored the reform, turned red-faced when the district was unofficially named after him.

Louise came to New Orleans to meet her fiancé, but she could never locate him. (Google Images)

Storyville became the city's experimental district for legalized prostitution. Fabulous bordellos, lavishly decorated, sprung up in the Storyville district.

Racial distinctions were still enforced, and no black males could patronize white bordellos and no black women could work in the white bordellos.

Much of the money made in Storyville came from the outrageous liquor prices charged in the bordellos.

Lulu White's Mahogany Hall catered to customers who could meet her high prices, as did others, such as Josie Arlington's bordello. Tom Anderson, the unofficial mayor of Storyville, owned the largest saloon in Storyville and shares in others.

There were hundreds of "crib" girls who charged lower rates and worked out of small two-room cribs with only a bed and a chair. The crib girls paid about three dollars a night for a crib and then charged their male customers anywhere from ten to fifty cents. The heavy competition kept prices low in the cribs.

Storyville was conveniently located next to the main railroad passenger terminal. As men got off the trains, they were handed the Blue Books that advertised the whores and their specialties. The Blue Books did not mention prostitution or sex, but the message was clear.

One such book printed the title "Blue Book" at the top. At the bottom was printed "Tenderloin 400". This book contained portraits and descriptions of the better-known madams, such as Lulu White, Josie Arlington, and Willie Piazza.

In the Mae West movie, "Belle of the Nineties," Mae West's character was reportedly modeled after Lulu White. Lulu wore diamonds on all her fingers and a wig of wild red hair.

Popular bordello madam Josie Arlington became involved with Philip Lobrano while only seventeen years old. He introduced Josie into the world of sporting houses, or brothels.

Josie was smart and cool headed. She had a good instinct for business. She first opened the Chateau Lobrano d'Arlington. Later, she had a bordello simply called "Arlington".

She made enough money that she went on to buy an expensive mansion on Esplanade Avenue. She also purchased a lavish tomb for herself in the town's historic cemetery.

In 1917, the Department of the Navy closed down Storyville, saying it was a threat to national security. On the eve of World War One, a military base opened in New Orleans and it was illegal for prostitution to operate within five miles of a base.

The city eventually razed most of the district to build a housing development. Most of Storyville's buildings were lost.

Louise the Unfortunate

It is said Louise came to Natchez to be married. She arrived by steamboat, landing at "Under-the-Hill", a very busy but rowdy section of Natchez. She was never able to locate her fiancé.

Her story grows even fuzzier. One tale is that Louise remained in Natchez, even though she couldn't find her fiancé. Another version is that her finance had died and she lacked funds to return home.

After working at various respectable jobs, such as a waitress, seamstress, and housekeeper, Louise eventually became a "Woman of the Night" at one of the many brothels.

Some say a Doctor who had treated her paid for her funeral. Another story is that a wealthy plantation owner who had frequented her parlor paid her funeral expenses.

Whatever Louise's story, she gained someone's attention. She is buried in the Natchez cemetery with a headstone. There is no date on the stone.

Chapter 11

Jennie Rogers

Jennie Rogers' real name was Leah J. Fries and she was considered the most beautiful woman in Denver's red light district.

She let herself be seen by the Denver socialites as well. Each day, a carriage, pulled by a matching team of gray horses, was brought around to her door. She spent the next hour driving through the streets of Denver, including the richest part of the residential section.

Jenny Rogers
Colorado Historical Society

Jennie was a six-foot-tall brunette, statuesque and quite attractive. She was also hot-tempered, authoritative, skilled in business dealings, and not given to profanities.

She was seldom seen without her emerald earrings. The *Denver Times*, on September 25, 1886, ran an article concerning the filing of larceny charges against one "Edward Washington (colored)" for stealing "some diamonds from Jennie Rogers, on Holladay Street."

Clark Secrest, author of *Hell's Belles, Prostitution, Vice, and Crime in Early Denver*, said Washington was believed to be Jennie's houseman, but that the important point in the newspaper article was the fact her identity was given simply as "*Jennie Rogers , on Holladay Street.*"

Born in Allegheny, Pennsylvania, Jennie associated with farm produce peddlers. Because of her beauty, she is said to have entertained many offers of marriage.

According to her biography at the Colorado Historical Society, Jennie was married about 1860 to a physician by the name of Fries. She soon ran away with a steamboat captain whose craft was named the *Jennie Rogers.*

She next became housekeeper for a Pittsburgh mayor. According to author Secrest, "The ensuing scandal prompted her departure from Pittsburgh with enough hush money to establish in St. Louis her first fashionable resort."

Jennie advertised her new parlor house by driving her boarding girls about town in a coach drawn by four horses. Jennie, herself, was an excellent horsewoman.

She next moved to Denver where all the new silver strikes were taking place. She found Mattie Silks had already been there for three years. Jennie bought her first Denver parlor house at 527 Holladay Street from Mattie for four-thousand-six-hundred-dollars.

The first thing Jennie did to her new whorehouse was to get rid of all the old furnishings and re-paper the walls. Her parlor was sheer elegance.

Instead of keeping the doors and windows closed as did most parlor houses, Jennie opened them up, letting out the stale air that was fouled with a mixture of perfume, alcohol and tobacco.

Jennie put bars on the windows to discourage robberies, as well as to stop the practice of some of her "boarders" from allowing men to enter through the windows to conduct business.

Jennie married John Wood, a bartender at the Brown Palace Hotel. He was fourteen-years her junior, but the marriage was short lived. She caught him tom-catting with another woman. She shot her pistol at him but the erring husband

Jennie Rogers in her sixties. (Colorado State Archives)

suffered only a flesh wound. The irate Jennie filed for, and got, a speedy divorce.

89

She next built a fine parlor at 1950 Market Street in Denver, only five blocks from the meeting places of the Colorado legislature. David Mechling owned a drug store between Jennie's parlor house and the legislative halls.

Mechling said when the legislature was in session, about three o'clock in the afternoon the lawmakers would adjourn to Jennie's place to amuse themselves.

Her parlor house had fifteen bedrooms and one of the first centralized furnaces in town. She employed twenty-two "boarders" there at one time.

As Jennie grew older, she suffered from Bright's disease, a disease of the kidneys, which took away much of her good looks.

She summoned her lawyer, Stanley C. Warner, to her residence at 1950 Market Street to prepare a will. She left everything to her sister, Annie Smith; a niece, Annie Prestle; and a nephew, Marsh Mariner.

She grew increasingly ill and died October 17, 1909.

Chapter 12

Saving a Bawdy House

When the fire broke out in Pat Logan's saloon in the unkempt mining camp first called Sears Diggings, men rushed from all directions to douse the blaze.

The volunteer firemen in the California mining camp literally loved a fire. Kegs of beer were placed at strategic locations to help squelch the thirst that accompanied the fighting of a fire. Fighting fire then became a pleasure and the men became more enthusiastic with each drink.

It was at the height of such a fire in the gold camp that someone remembered Madame Touvounties and her *bawdy house* lay in the path of the fire. The men simply could not bear to see Madame Touvounties and her lovely girls put out of business.

The men in the camp considered Madame Touvounties establishment as irreplaceable. It was as much an asset to the community as the bank and the hardware store. When the firemen realized time was growing short, they knew they must take action, and do it quickly.

Filling and quickly emptying their beer mugs, the firemen settled on a solution. The volunteers converged on Madame Touvounties establishment and formed muscular lines on each side of the building.

At a barked signal, the firemen picked up the building and carried it safely away from the advancing flames.

Madame Touvounties and her girls were properly impressed and promised special privileges once the fire was out. Some say those special privileges never actually materialized, but the firemen reasoned that it was the thought that counted.

There were other incidents that caused the gold camp some notoriety. The gold camp was first called Sears Diggings, after a sea captain by the name of Sears. Captain Sears had brought a ship with passengers to San Francisco in 1850, when the California Gold Rush was still in its heyday.

He joined the throng of passengers that immediately headed for the gold fields, leaving his craft to rot in the mud flats of Yerba Buena (San Francisco). Sears was as much a greenhorn at gold mining as were the majority of others who rushed headstrong to the gold fields.

While in Nevada City, Sears heard a man known as "Crazy Stoddard" tell a wild-eyed tale of having discovered a lake of gold, but was chased away by a band of warlike Indians.

An expedition was organized to follow Stoddard back to his fabulous discovery. Sears decided to trail along. The expedition was soon abandoned, as the miners accompanying Stoddard grew disgusted with the venture when no such lake of gold appeared.

Sears began walking back alone to the Yuba. He wandered onto a ridge that now bears his name. He decided to search for gold at Slate Creek. He soon found color in considerable quantity.

After harvesting several ounces, his mistake was letting his friends in on his find. These friends couldn't help but blare the information of Sear's find up and down the river.

Before long, all the visible gold and all the easy pickings were gone. The friends that descended on Sears' find were as incompetent at prospecting as was Sears. None of them had learned the basic rudiments of placer mining.

One member of the group was a surly man named Gibson, who had a reputation as a loud mouth, a man of questionable ethics, and a brawler. One miner said Gibson couldn't "be trusted with an anvil, as he would find some way to slip it in his pocket and walk away with it".

Gibson soon wandered over a ridge and set to prospecting on his own. Unlike Sears, Gibson kept his new find secret, and struck it rich. The camp that developed was called Gibsonville.

Chapter 13

The Klondike Girls

When the gold strike hit the Klondike, the miners simply couldn't spend their money fast enough. They gambled on anything, making outrageous wagers. Two old-timers bet ten-thousand-dollars on their spitting accuracy, using a crack in the wall as a bulls eye.

Bartenders quickly learned to let their fingernails grow long. When they scooped gold dust into the scales, enough gold gathered under their long fingernails to augment their income handsomely.

The prostitutes also prospered. Diamond Tooth Gerty said, "The poor ginks have just gotta spend it. They're scared they'll die before they have it all out of the ground."

The Klondike's dance halls and saloons invented a voucher system on which to pay the ladies. Every dollar spent by a miner being entertained by a dance hall girl earned an ivory disk.

Discovery City on Otter Creek was built in a couple of months. The two women pictured began a cafe, bakery and lodging business. (UAF Archives)

The girls stashed these vouchers in their stockings. As the music blared, the prospectors were happy to spend their money as they danced waltzes, polkas, schottisches and square dances. Come morning, their legs lumpy with vouchers, the ladies cashed in their ivory disks.

The dance hall women usually disguised their true identities with colorful aliases. They were as well known for these trademarks or physical attributes, as for their names.

Besides the usual Sweet Marie, Ping Pong, or Caprice, there was "The Grizzly Bear", who weighed one-hundred-seventy pounds. She was missing one eye. Rumor said it had been torn from its socket in a brawl with another dance hall queen.

96

Not all the women in the Klondike were dance hall queens. Mrs. Bessie Thomas felt women were as entitled to work in the gold rush as men.

"Miners have got to eat and I think there is more money to be made in feeding them than in slaving my life away here. I have got to earn my own living, and I do not see why there shouldn't be just as good a chance for me in a mining camp as there is for a man."

Harriet Pullen left her husband and children in Washington state hoping to improve her life with the gold rush. When she arrived in Skagway in 1897, Harriet began to bake apple pies in pie tins made from discarded cans, using dried apples that most miners carried.

She made enough money that she sent for her three sons as well as her team of horses so she could go into the freighting business on the White Pass Trail.

Klondike Kate's real name was Kathleen Eloisa Rockwell. She claimed to have come to the Klondike as a means of supporting her mother, who had divorced with no means of making a living.

Kate was considered just another actress when she arrived in the Klondike. She gained a certain amount of fame by developing her "flame dance". For this dance, Kate came on stage wearing an elaborate dress covered in red sequins and an enormous cape.

She flung off her cape, revealing a cane that was attached to 200 yards of red chiffon. She leaped and twirled the chiffon until she looked as though fire was blazing around her.

Klondike Kate went to the Klondike to support her mother. (Google Images)

The miners loved it. She was a hit and the miners called her "The Flame of the Yukon".

Kate fell for a man named Alexander Pantages. He convinced her to help him buy a string of theaters in the Pacific Northwest and start their own theater company.

She was for the plan, but she wanted to do it as man and wife. Kate and Pantages traveled a lot in 1902. It was during one of these trips that she found out he had married a violinist and taken all of her money. She never forgave him.

Kate eventually settled in Oregon where she worked at odd jobs to support herself. She later clung to her "Belle of the Klondike" reputation, even handing out postcards to people with her photo. She died in 1957.

Chapter 14

'Madame Moustache'

Eleanor Dumont
(Mercaldo Archives)

When she stepped down from the stage in Nevada City in 1854, all heads, both men and women, turned in her direction.

She appeared to be in her early twenties and her activities mystified residents of the mining town for days. She was neatly and stylishly dressed, and looked fresh even after her grueling stage ride.

Miners cast admiring glances at this classy-appearing lady. They couldn't figure out what a young woman like her would be doing in a rough and tumble town like Nevada City, California.

Some surmised the lady might be the town's new schoolteacher. Others thought she came to join a fiancée. Others thought even worse, that she might be a madam, or was looking for such a person for whom to work.

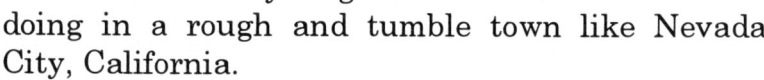

Two young miners jumped at the chance to carry her bags into Fepp's Hotel, where she registered as "Eleanora Dumont".

For days the elegant Madame Eleanora Dumont wandered up and down dusty Broad Street, the main street in Nevada City, peering into windows of shops that had gone out of business. Her activity only increased the curiosity of the miners as well as that of the few wives of miners living in the mining town.

Commented one woman, "There's got to be some bad in a girl with all her charms who seems to have nothing to do but strut up and down Main Street."

Finally, the mystery of Eleanor Dumont came out in the open. It happened when she handed a printing order to Editor Wait of the *Nevada Journal*.

"I want this handbill printed and distributed to every man in this town to let them know I am opening the best gambling emporium in northern California," she told the editor.

Soon after, the charming Eleanor opened "Vingt-et-Un" (French for twenty-one). It was a finely furnished and carpeted gambling saloon for only well-behaved and well-groomed men.

Madame Dumont served champagne instead of whiskey, and she dealt the cards herself. It didn't take her miner clientele long to observe that Miss Dumont knew her gambling profession well.

The smitten miners regularly lost their hard-earned gold pokes earned from their day in the mines to the deft-fingered Miss Dumont. She seldom lost her deals or her demure smile as she collected the miner's gold. They seemed to think it a privilege just to be in her presence.

Gold production fell off in 1855 in Nevada City. Some felt the diggings there were worked out. It worried Eleanor Dumont, who considered closing the Vingt-et-Un.

About this time, Lucky Dan Tobin, a card sharp and professional gambler rolled into town. He was footloose at the time and looking for a place to light.

Not only did he like the gambling house of Madame Dumont, but he liked its proprietor as well. She and Tobin joined forces. He brought in poker tables, a keno operation, chuck-a-luck and a faro bank. He hired more dealers and added a small band of violinists to entertain the gamblers.

Madame Dumont had made some stipulations, most of which Tobin ignored. But one which she insisted upon was that women would be barred from the premises.

As far as anyone knew, Eleanor Dumont had no lovers. She kept her personal life private.

The new diversified entertainment worked and the gambling house became profitable again, helped by the fact that another boom had arrived in the surrounding gold fields.

It was during her second year in Nevada City that close observers saw the unflattering growth of hair on her upper lip. Because of this, she was given the equally unflattering name, *"Madame Moustache"*. Soon, it seemed, miners came to see the mustachioed lady as much as they did to gamble.

In time, Eleanor sold her Nevada City gambling emporium and began wandering through the gold country. She drifted throughout the mining camps of the western territories, spending time in Deadwood, South Dakota, and in mining camps in Montana, Idaho and Nevada.

Eleanor Dumont became notorious throughout the west. One story tells about her being accosted by two drunks as she walked home one dark night.

"We'll take your purse," one growled.

"No, you'll not," she calmly informed the pair.

One of the robbers held a gun on her, telling her she had better hand over her purse, or else. She reached under her skirt as if to pull out her purse, but instead brought out a derringer.

Firing point blank, she killed one man and the other disappeared into the night.

Natural aging eventually replaced the youthful charms of Eleanor Dumont. She put on weight and her once hourglass figure turned plump.

Even worse, her moustache turned even more prominent, darkening her upper lip. Her gambling skill had left her and she soon turned to prostitution. She maintained a *"bawdy"* house in Bannock, Montana, at one time.

Some say that one of her girls in that enterprise was Martha Jane Cannary, better known as *"Calamity Jane."* Eleanor then moved on to San Francisco to try her luck, but that venture failed.

At one point, she gave up her fast-paced gambling and prostitution ways and settled down on a ranch in eastern Nevada. She married a small-time gambler and made the mistake of turning over her savings to him. He squandered her money and disappeared.

The once-beautiful Eleanor Dumont eventually showed up in Bodie, the "toughest town in the west." She struggled to survive and soon became an object of pity by the townspeople.

On September 13, 1879, the Aurora, Nevada, *Esmeralda Herald* carried an obituary, noting that the body of a woman was found two miles south of Bodie and was identified as that of Eleanor Dumont, more familiarly known as *"Madame Moustache."*

The gamblers and bartenders who had known Eleanor saw to it that she had a decent burial in a good cemetery, rather than in a pauper's grave.

Chapter 15

The Bordello Lure

What is it that brings women into the *bawdy house* business, asked a U.S. Senate committee investigating the matter.

A bordello girl supplied some of the answers. "You're looking for the things that made such women as I?". Low wages! Dance halls! Hunger! Cold! They all helped a bit, but they didn't turn the trick themselves.

"You're all a bunch of hypocrites," she fired at the committee, "afraid to look the thing in its face and afraid to learn the truth. I don't know any girls who sold themselves for money to buy bread or clothes, but I do know lots of us who hit the road for hell because a lot of blackguards kept hounding us with their rotten 'attentions'.

"God help the men and not us. We're all right when we start—all we need is to be let alone. There are hundreds and hundreds of kids and sports who hang around State Street (Chicago) and wait like wolves for the tired girls to leave the stores."

In her book, *Daughters of Joy, Sisters of Misery,* Anne M. Butler characterized the typical bordello inmate as "homeless and youthful—ages fifteen to thirty."

The reckless life of the bordello woman is depicted in this photo within a parlor house.   (Colorado Historical Society)

The author noted that some *bawdy houses* prided themselves on offering young virgins for defloration, while other madams were just as proud to boast that a young girl had never been ruined in her house.

These young girls were either runaways or expelled from home by their parents. When exciting tales of glitter and glamour are placed before these youngsters, who are often uneducated, the lure is more understandable.

One young woman that arrived in Denver from Wyoming, sought help at finding a job from an employment office. She was advised by the agency interviewer to adopt a course of *vice*. Luckily, one of the people she was referred to was Verona Baldwin, a madam.

Verona quizzed the young girl and found out that she truly was an innocent. Verona now had a chance to warn a young girl of the error of entering the world of prostitution.

Verona Baldwin called the police, and Detectives McIlduff and Burlew took the girl to police headquarters and later to Union Station to catch a train home. The police paid for the train ticket.

In her memoir, Madam Nell Kenball, who kept houses in St. Louis, New Orleans, and San Francisco, wrote: "Hookers are mean but sentimental. They cry over dogs, kittens, kids, novels, and songs."

Ice cream parlors were especially favorite places for procurers to pick up young girls and induce them to enter the world of prostitution. The refreshment parlors seemed like safe places to the young girl from out of town, not knowing what to do next.

Another source for madams to entice new personnel into the *bawdy houses* was divorce courts. Alimony was rarely asked for and even more rarely granted. This made a penniless young divorcee (or a girl off the farm) almost certain to be approached by a procurer.

Clark Secrest, in his book *Hell's Belles, Prostitution, Vice, and Crime in Early Denver* described one procedure used for obtaining new girls for a brothel.

A presentable young procurer would strike up an acquaintance with a girl and court her. Eventually, she would acquiesce to accompany him to bed, but he might first have to promise to marry her.

Sometimes a bogus marriage ceremony would be performed. The couple would then retire to a hotel room for their "honeymoon". When she awoke the next morning, she would find her suitor gone and that she was actually in a brothel room.

The girl would be kept a virtual prisoner there, cajoled, sometimes drugged and raped until her spirit was broken and she agreed to work as instructed.

The *Denver Times* described an incident where a Mrs. F. C. Probasco needed to borrow some money. Knowing no place else to go, she finally went to Nellie White, the keeper of a bagnio on Market Street.

Nellie was willing to advance the money, but demanded some sort of security. After a conference, the troubled Mrs. Probasco went away, soon to return with a sixteen-year-old-girl, Florence Loew.

"Here she is," said Mrs. Probasco. "Now give me the five-dollars."

Florence Loew left the brothel within a week because it was "so utterly repugnant". Police learned of the transaction and arrested Mrs.

Probasco's husband, the architect of the scheme. Florence had been a family friend of the Probascos.

Denver physician George W. Cox commented on the character of Denver prostitutes.

"Generally speaking, the behavior of a 'thoroughbred' prostitute is of the most vicious and disgusting character. Influenced by their associates and surroundings, they very soon lose all the native modesty they may have possessed, and acquire habits of indolence, filthiness, dishonesty and intemperance.

"Smoking, chewing, dipping snuff, drinking, eating opium and fighting all seem to follow as natural consequences of the depraved way of living.

Almost without exception they are of a roving disposition—moving about from city to city, and from house to house in the same city—and part of their religion seems to be to skip on a board bill or to leave an unliquidated debt at the dress-maker's.

"This last named trait may be partly owing to the fact that they are always bankrupt."

Dr. Cox placed the life span of prostitutes at eight to fifteen years after commencing their career.

Chapter 16

Cattle Kate

When Ella Watson first arrived in Rawlins, Wyoming, she worked at the Rawlins House. She worked as a cook and a domestic for two years. Because the establishment was thought to be a brothel, she was labeled a prostitute.

Jim Averell was a homesteader, who opened a general store and saloon near the Oregon and Mormon trails.

During his trips to Rawlins, Jim and Ella Watson, who later became known as "Cattle Kate," became infatuated with each other. The couple traveled to Lander, Wyoming, presumably to get married.

Ella "Cattle Kate" Watson was lynched by a group of Wyoming cattlemen who claimed she was rustling cattle from them.
(University of Wyoming)

It is unclear whether a marriage ever took place. Many think the trip to Lander was in order for Kate to file for a homestead near that of Jim Averell's.

Because only one homestead per family was permitted, it is likely that Jim and Ella never really got married.

Dubbed as "Cattle Kate" by a newspaper, Kate's cattle herd kept growing at a mysterious rate.

Neighboring cattlemen believed admiring cowboys in Averell's saloon were receiving personal favors from Kate in exchange for beef on the hoof, beef that belonged to the ranchers.

Jim Averell
(Wyoming State Museum)

In the fall of 1888, Ella bought twenty head of footsore cattle from a trail driver. When she applied for a brand, her application was rejected for unknown reasons. Kate then bought an existing brand, the **L U** from another rancher. She then branded the twenty cattle she had bought from the trail driver.

On July 20, 1889 a stock detective named George Henderson rode through Ella's pasture and saw cattle with the **L U** brand.

He notified Albert Bothwell, a wealthy cattle rancher that neighbored Ella's property. Many people believed that Bothwell knew that Ella had acquired her cattle a year earlier. Still, he seized on the situation as a chance to get rid of Jim Averell and Ella Watson.

Albert John Bothwell was a neighbor of Ella. He wanted her land and water rights. He approached Ella several times with offers, but she invariably refused.

Bothwell had run-ins, too, with Jim Averell, even though the homesteader had given the rancher a right of way through his property that allowed Bothwell to irrigate his pastureland.

Based on what detective Henderson had told him, Bothwell called for a meeting of the Wyoming Stock Growers Association to discuss the newly-branded cattle on Ella's property. Six of the stockmen decided to take matters into their own hands. Other cattlemen wanted nothing to do with it.

Claiming they had warrants to arrest them, the six ranchers converged on Jim's roadhouse and took Ella and Jim captive. The six ranchers were A.J. Bothwell, John Durbin, Robert Conner, E.F. McLean, Tom Sun, and a man named Galbrath. The couple was hung from a tree near the Sweetwater River.

According to her grand nephew, Daniel W. (Watson) Brumbaugh, little of what has been written about Cattle Kate is true.

"There have been several books and magazine articles written about Ella Watson, said Brumbaugh. "Several of these authors never really researched her life. They just took what the newspapers said about her in the days of her lynching for granted and wrote about her from the articles."

Brumbaugh was especially critical of the newspaper in Cheyenne, Wyoming. "The newspaper at that time belonged to the powerful organization known as the Wyoming Stock Growers Association. They controlled the newspaper and the printing."

"They printed what they wanted the public to hear, not the real facts about her life and what really took place at her lynching. They fabricated the lives of three women into one. The editor of the Cheyenne newspaper wrote the incident like you would a dime store novel."

Brumbaugh said Ella's own father told her siblings never to speak of her name again after he attended her inquest in Wyoming in August 1889.

Not one of them ever spoke of her name after that, he said, even to their own children, though some of them tried to get their parents to tell them about their oldest aunt.

Brumbaugh, however, could not let the issue rest. "I have been on the homestead site in Smith County, Kansas that her father homesteaded in November 1877 where Ella lived until she married. I have traveled to Rawlins, Wyoming where she filed for her claim. I have researched in the local courthouse in that city for her records.

"I have been to the homestead site on the Pathfinder Ranch and the lynching site and seen the tree from which the cattlemen lynched her and Jim Averell. I have sent off to the National Archives for her homestead filings. I do know something about her life since I am related to her."

Brumbaugh added, "Only one of the lynchers knew Ella Watson well. He lived within a mile of Ella's homestead place. He lied and fabricated stories about Jim and Ella so he could get rid of them and finally get their land and water rights."

According to her Estate Administrator, the cattle did belong to her, and he sued the Durbin Cattle Company and A.J. Bothwell for compensation for her estate, said Brumbaugh.

He detailed Ella's early life:

"Ella Liddy Watson was born out of wedlock in July 1860. Her mother Frances was born in Dromore, County Down Ireland, and came to Canada with her parents and her other siblings around 1858. Since they were pure Irish, the fact of an unwed mother probably brought shame upon the family at that time.

"On February 24, 1886, Ella was going towards the courthouse in Rawlins, when she met this handsome young man. He introduced himself as James Averell. He told her he had a roadhouse that had an eating place and a general store. He also had a bar where cowboys or anybody else could have a drink. He told Ella about some land adjoining his that she could probably homestead."

Ella Watson and Jim Averell later drove to Lander, Wyoming and applied for a marriage license. The marriage license was never returned. Years later, after the lynching, John Fales, a neighbor of Ella, said the couple was engaged. They intended to get married after Ella proved up on her homestead claim.

After the hanging, the bodies of Ella and Jim were brought back to Jim's roadhouse. They were buried on Jim's ranch.

Was Ella Watson a prostitute? According to Jay Nash in his book, *Encyclopedia of Western Lawmen and Outlaws,* "Ella was known to many men other than Averell, having earned her living as a prostitute in Denver, Cheyenne, and Rawlins.

When the six accused ranchers were brought before a grand jury, the case was not heard because of a lack of witnesses. The only witness, a young boy, was killed a few weeks before the scheduled hearing.

While circumstantial evidence certainly points a finger at the six cattlemen as the murderers of Jim Averell and Ella Watson, it is unlikely that conclusive evidence will ever materialize. The case still lives in the minds of many in Wyoming.

Chapter 17

Timber Kate

Kate's life was a depressing one from any standpoint. She was part of a notorious saloon act with her female lover, Bella Rawhide.

The two performed live sex acts on stage in honky-tonks throughout the west, including Carson City, Nevada, Spokane, Washington, and Cheyenne, Wyoming.

Young Bella then fell head-over-heels in love with a half-breed ruffian named Tug Daniels. The two ran off together, leaving Timber Kate without a partner.

Kate resorted to dressing as a man in white tights and lifting weights on stage. She usually ended her act by doing a strip-tease.

In 1880, Bella Rawhide and Tug Daniels met up with Kate in Carson City at the Bee Hive Whorehouse on Quincy Street. There was a rowdy showdown, during which Tug Daniels pulled a knife and according to reports, slashed Kate "from her crotch to her navel."

Timber Kate died on the whorehouse floor. Tug Daniels disappeared and was never seen again.

In 1882, Bella Rawhide committed suicide by drinking cleaning fluid.

Chapter 18

Crazy Kate Shea

It was indeed a hot time in Crazy Kate Shea's one-story boarding and *bawdy house* on A Street in Virginia City, Nevada. It was so hot, that most of the town burned.

The *Territorial Enterprise* headlined the damage:

VIRGINIA CITY IN RUINS

The newspaper pegged the immediate loss to the city at seven million dollars.

"It was soon seen that the efforts of the firemen to control the flames would be fruitless, and the people began to assert themselves to save their goods," the newspaper reported.

Kate Shea's *bawdy house,* where the fire started, housed five male boarders, three prostitutes, and Kate herself. However, Kate was known to work out of other brothels, and on this particular night, worked at Nellie Sayers brothel on C Street.

The fire apparently started when someone at Crazy Kate's house knocked over a kerosene lamp. A strong wind was blowing and the westward part of the city turned into a sea of flames.

Brothels lined up on D Street in Virginia City.
(Mark Twain Book Store)

The newspaper said street people were seen lugging trunks, articles of furniture and bundles of bedding and clothing. "No sooner had they deposited their loads in what was supposed to be a place of safety than the advancing flames compelled them to make another retreat."

"Many persons thus moved their goods from six to eight times, their pile growing less at each

122

interval till at last they found themselves left with a mere handful of property."

Crazy Kate denied she had anything to do with the fire. She had the following statement printed in the *Territorial Enterprise* (edited for readability):

"The impression having gone abroad that I am the cause of the desolating fire of the 26th will the citizens of Virginia hear my story sustained by witnesses.

"On the morning of the fire several persons, some of whose names are appended, were sleeping in my house on A Street. Those in the basement awakened, suffocating with smoke smelling of kerosene, which seemed to have been spread over the fuel and kindling under the basement and fired.

"I was asleep in the second story of my house when the fire broke out, and escaped through a window. No drunken carousal as reported, was carried on in my house the night preceding the fire. I never broke a lighted lamp intentionally by kicking, throwing it, or otherwise. If I am 'Crazy Kate Shea', this community owes me their Sympathy." (signed) Kate Shea.

Virginia City residents quickly began to rebuild. Some of the prostitutes recovered as well, and many of them took possession of their old quarters. But for most prostitutes, things were not good in Virginia City. Beatings of the women became so common-place that in February, 1877, a law was passed to "prevent cruelty to women in the State of Nevada."

This law would punish men who beat women by tying the men to a post in a public place and embarrass them. The law read:

> *Section 2. Any male person in the State who is more than eighteen years of age, who shall willfully and violently strike, beat, or torture the body of any maiden or woman who is more than sixteen years of age, shall be deemed guilty of a misdemeanor, and upon conviction in any court of competent jurisdiction, shall be sentenced to be firmly tied or lashed in a standing posture to the post or pillar described in section one of the Act, and shall be kept in such tied and standing posture for a period not less than two hours nor more than ten hours in the daytime of any day.*

The law declared that a placard with the words, "Woman beater" or "Wife beater", in large Roman characters, be attached to the breast garments of the accused.

124

Even though the law was passed, beatings continued. A month after the law had been passed, a girl ran crying to Judge Moses' court room, begging officers to stop her father from killing her mother.

She led the officers to her house. The beaten woman was in her last stages of pregnancy and the father had beaten and kicked her until she was unconscious and unable to rise.

The wife-beating law that had been passed a month earlier was not used.

The first time the law was used was in the case of James McCarthy, who brutally beat his wife in Carson City. When the sheriff arrived, Mrs. McCarthy was lying on the floor in a pool of blood. She had been severely beaten and suffered a head wound through to her skull.

At the trial, she vouched for her husband, saying they had both been drinking.

The court, however, ordered James McCarthy be tied to a post in a public place with a placard reading "Wife Beater" pinned to his breast. A large crowd gathered for the occasion.

McCarthy's attorney claimed the sentence was unconstitutional and the punishment too severe and cruel.

McCarthy was released to return to his loving, forgiving wife.

Chapter 19

Julia Moore

It didn't pay to fool around with Julia Moore. While she was born to a respectable family in the eastern United States, she couldn't resist the life of the west.

Julia made her way to Grass Valley where she married Frank Moore. It was when she moved to Virginia City that all her past troubles were laid bare.

In Virginia City, she was immediately involved in a fist fight that turned into a shooting. The fight occurred among a group of boisterous revelers at Harry Gribben's New York Shades on South C. Street.

Madame Julia Moore got into an argument with a woman named Louise. Julia drew her pistol, but the gun was taken away from her. After she had calmed down, her gun was returned to her.

When the ruckus started again and Johnny Clark, the saloon keeper, attempted to restore order, Julia shot him in the groin.

Julia was arrested and fined two-thousand-dollars. It was then that her past caught up with her. It came out that Julia had married Frank Moore in Grass Valley, California. Frank, it was said, had raped a Mrs. Martha Taylor in the mining town of Rough and Ready. He had also killed twenty-seven-year-old Alexander McClanahan, the Foreign Miner Tax Collector.

For this offense, Frank was sentenced to hang June 19, 1857. Julia went to his cell on the eve of the hanging to see her husband. After she left, Frank asked his jailor for a glass of wine. A few minutes later, the jailor heard him groaning.

Frank had poisoned himself, robbing the three-thousand people that showed up for his hanging from seeing the grand spectacle.

An investigation noted that Julia was the last person to see her husband. When she was accused of giving him the poison, she denied it, and showed authorities where Frank had stuck the poison to the bottom of a chair with candle wax.

Madame Moore couldn't stay out of trouble. She was soon arrested for larceny, tried and acquitted. A short time later, she was again arrested, this time on a charge of aiding in an abortion in which the mother died.

Chapter 20

Cock-Eyed Liz

She arrived in Buena Vista with a flourish, drawing the attention of miners, teamsters and everyone else in town.

Three large trunks were unloaded from the baggage car and she carried a carpet bag as well as a hat box. Her painted face announced her intentions to everyone around her.

At the hotel, she registered as Lizzie Spurgen. After disposing of her luggage, Lizzie asked to be shown town lots that might be for sale. On the north side of main street, just west of the courthouse, she found what she wanted.

She let it be known that she had come to Colorado because of her health. She was an asthmatic and suffered from frequent bouts of bronchitis. She thought the clean, pure Colorado air would ease her discomfort.

She built a one-story brick house on the lot she had selected. She called it a "Palace of Joy."

In her three trunks, Lizzie had packed a number of taffeta and silken gowns that even surpassed the elegant clothes in which she arrived. If her clothes didn't give her away, her makeup did.

"No respectable woman in Colorado would be seen with the least touch of makeup," town mongers whispered. Lizzie wasn't bothered.

The parlor of her new house was on the right, just inside the entrance. The house had enough rooms to accommodate four girls, beside herself.

Cock-Eyed Liz's house became a center of Buena Vista night life. Her four "boarders" just seemed to materialize out of nowhere. Neither Lizzie nor the girls talked about their pasts.

Drawing depicting Cock-Eye Liz (Colorado Historical

Lizzie was twenty-nine years old, and stood five-foot-seven-inches tall. She was a handsome woman except for one thing, one eye over which she had little control.

An accident had caused permanent damage to one eye, leading to the inhospitable nickname of "Cock-Eyed Liz", given to the otherwise striking lady.

There were different stories as to what had actually happened to Liz. One story, printed in Caroline Bancroft's book, *Six Racy Madams of Colorado,* was that a competing madam, Belle Brown, resented Lizzie's success.

This is the former parlor house of Cock-Eyed Liz in Buena Vista, Colorado.
(Colorado Historical Society)

She is said to have gotten a group of the town's worst brawlers roaring drunk one night and sent them to Liz's to stir up trouble.

Some say that during the ensuing row, Lizzie Spurgen was hit in one eye and blinded. She lost both the sight and the muscular control of the eye, which occasioned the nickname, "Cock-Eyed Liz".

Customers paid three dollars to be entertained by one of Liz's girls. It is not known how much Madam Liz kept for herself. She did like to advertise her handsome "boarders". She would sometimes pay five-dollars to rent a two-seated buggy and take her girls for a ride around town.

One of Lizzie's "boarders" that left a deep impression on her customers was "Pancake Fan". She was said to be soft as a pancake. What impressed people, however, was the fact that she left the bordello business and went straight, taking a job with the Salvation Army in Salt Lake City.

On FrontierNet's web site, Lizzie is reported to have lamented to her housekeeper:

> *I'll have to pay for the awful things I've done, won't I? I was married when I was thirteen years old to a man old enough to be my father. He put me in a "house" and made me become one of "the girls". I used to run away, but he would always find me and bring me back. He would beat me so badly, that I finally gave up. Years later I became a madam. I couldn't help myself when I was young, but, oh, all the little lives I've destroyed—that's what I'll have to pay for—all those little young lives.*

On a lighter note, Lizzie used to say, "A parlor house is where the girls go to look for a husband and the husbands go to look for a girl."

Her humor showed through in other ways. For instance, she kept a pet magpie in a cage on the front lawn. She trained the bird to greet each passerby with:

"Come in, Boys! Come in!"

One day, the bird escaped and a neighborhood boy threw a rock at it, breaking the bird's leg. Lizzie rushed the bird to a veterinarian, but the leg had to be amputated.

Nevertheless, the bird still hopped about on one leg, announcing to passersby:

"Come in, Boys! Come in!"

Lizzie's Palace of Joy had one frequent visitor. This was Alphonse Enderlin, a Buena Vista plumber, with the unusual nickname of "Foozy".

A story told in Bancroft's *Six Racy Madams of Colorado*, is that one Sunday morning, Foozy drove up to Lizzie's Palace of Joy in a buggy. This was unusual in that he usually drove a buckboard in which he carried his plumbing and building tools.

Foozy wanted Lizzie to ride over to Fairplay, Colorado and spend the night, saying she needed a change. It was an all-day drive, but it turned out to be the nicest day Liz could remember.

To cap off the otherwise magnificent day, Foozy suggested that they get married the following morning. The wedding took place, with Lizzie giving her age as "over-twenty-one" (Her real age was forty-one). Foozy gave his age as thirty-five, making Liz six years older than him, a trifle that concerned her briefly.

Cock-Eyed Liz gave up her Palace of Joy, letting her girls move to other brothels. Foozy built a clapboard wing onto Liz's brick house. This wing was turned into two apartments, which the couple rented out to supplement their income.

One evening, Foozy was playing poker with some men in the back room of the pool hall. A traveling salesman dropped in to watch the game, chattering away all the time.

At one point he asked, "Whatever happened to Cock-Eyed Liz who used to own a sporting house here?"

The room grew dead-quiet. The only calm person at the table was Foozy. He simply replied, "I married her."

The salesman left, and the rest of the men simply renewed their card playing without another mention of the incident.

Liz and Foozy's marriage lasted thirty-one years. In 1929, Liz's heart gave out. Foozy buried the love of his life in the Mt. Olivet cemetery. Five years later, he again rejoined her.

This headstone covers both the graves of Cock-Eyed Liz Enderlin and her husband "Foozy" Enderlin.

(Colorado Historical Society)

Chapter 21

Lottie Johl

Lottie Johl
(Bodie State Park)

It is not known when or where Lottie Johl became a prostitute. What is known is that she was born in Iowa in 1855.

Lottie did get married at a young age, had a daughter and then divorced her husband. It's not known what went wrong with the marriage.

After months of struggle, Lottie left her daughter, either with her parents or her ex-husband, and headed west. Tracing Lottie's past is difficult as no evidence exists regarding her surname.

It was in 1882, at age twenty-seven, that Lottie, the lone woman passenger, stepped off the stagecoach in Bodie, California.

Immediately, on arrival, she asked the stagecoach driver the direction to "Virgin Alley" or "Maiden Lane". One man, who heard her request, volunteered to show her the way. Both Virgin Alley and Maiden Lane were really one street and part of the red light district.

There was little doubt that she knew where she was going and for what purpose. It was an area of cribs, brothels and, too often, a place of desperation. Here is where women of all ages offer "love" for a price.

Lottie Johl's house.
(Bodie State Historic Park)

The *bawdy house girls* were not welcomed in Bodie during the day when the town's respected women might be doing their shopping.

Consequently, they kept to their seedy bordellos until the sun went down.

During the evening, the *bawdy house* ladies came out in their regal finery and whirled around the dance floor with their mining-prospector partners. They then might disappear abruptly into the area of cribs and brothels.

According to an account in *Soiled Doves, Prostitution in the Early West,* Anne Seagraves writes about Lottie and her Bodie experience.

"Lottie settled easily into the life of the rough mining town," wrote Seagraves. "She spent her days visiting with the other girls, and in the evening she joined in the excitement and bright lights of main street."

She loved to dance and became one of the most sought-after partners in Bodie. One night, while she was dancing, she noticed a large man in the dance hall watching her every move.

Eli Johl had fallen head over heels for the woman he thought was the handsomest person he had ever seen. Johl was a German immigrant and co-owner of one of Bodie's two butcher shops.

His partner in the butcher shop was Charles Donnelly. While Donnelly waited on customers, Johl did the dirty work of slaughtering and cutting up the meat that would go into the meat case.

After he saw Lottie in the dance hall, Eli began showering her with jewelry, money and attention. Her past and her present vocation did not matter to Johl. He had lost his heart to Lottie.

It was a new experience for Lottie. She had always been used by men, never showered with affection.

Lottie and Eli were married, and the proper women of Bodie were aghast at the happening. Perhaps the most distraught was the wife of the butcher shop's co-owner, Mrs. Donnelly, who was described as a haughty woman of English descent.

Mrs. Donnelly felt the marriage was a direct insult to her own social standing in the town of Bodie. She attempted to get the partnership between her husband and Eli Johl ended, without success.

Eli bought Lottie a house on Main Street, not far from the butcher shop. He filled it with the finest furnishings he could buy. Lottie was proud, both of her home and of her husband.

The couple decided to have a party. Eli sent carefully selected invitations to his friends. Lottie prepared a number of elegant dishes to serve.

When Mrs. Donnelly learned of the party, she discouraged all of her friends from attending. The night of the party was heart-breaking to Lottie. No one came to their party. Eli knew then that his wife would never be accepted in Bodie.

If anything, the occasion caused Eli and Lottie to grow closer. Eli was always greeted with a warm hug and a nice supper when he came home from the butcher shop.

Mrs. Donnelly was also Bodie's local artist. Her paintings were sold throughout Bodie, despite their somewhat questionable quality.

Eli watched Lottie as she grew lonelier and lonelier. He decided that if Mrs. Donnelly could paint, so could Lottie, and she probably could do it even better.

He purchased an easel, yards of canvas, paints and some expensive frames. Lottie's first attempts were not very good, but she did seem to show a certain flair for painting.

Her pictures soon covered all the walls of their home. But Eli wanted to see the paintings elsewhere as well. Like her party, her paintings were shunned by the Bodie townsfolk.

Eli had another plan. A masquerade ball was being held at the Miner's Union Hall. Eli sent to San Francisco for the finest gown he could buy. He was sure that when the people of Bodie got to know his wife, they would treat her more kindly.

The ball would be Lottie's coming-out party. Eli, however, would remain home. Lottie went alone to the ball. Her white satin gown glittered with artificial diamonds and pearls. Lottie was beautiful.

When the ball committee selected the winner of the most outstanding costume, it was given to the lady in the white satin gown. When the signal to unmask was given, the guests gasped.

Lottie's partner on the floor recognized her from her past reputation and walked off the floor, leaving her standing alone. Lottie ran from the hall in tears.

Eli raged like a wild bull when she came home in tears. Lottie, however, simply gave up on trying to gain the respect of the people in Bodie. The Johls grew closer because of the incident and kept to themselves.

One night, Lottie became ill. Eli sent for a doctor, who checked her over and prescribed some medicine. When Eli gave her the medicine, she became even more violently ill. Within twenty-four hours she was dead.

The people in Bodie believed she had committed suicide. Eli knew better and demanded an autopsy. The results showed that Lottie had been given poison by a mistake of the druggist who prepared her prescription.

The people's scorn wasn't finished. They refused to allow Lottie to be buried in the town's cemetery. She would have to be buried at the edge of the cemetery, just within the fence.

Eli built a memorial for his Lottie. He erected a high wrought-iron fence around her grave, the most elaborate in the cemetery.

Lottie's grave erected by Eli.

140

Chapter 22

Chicago Joe

Mary Welch arrived in New York from Ireland, with no money. She considered herself a resourceful woman, even though she was only fourteen-years of age.

The first thing she did was to change her name. She switched it to Josephine Airey, which she figured was more stylish. She worked at menial jobs in New York for awhile, but in a few years, she moved to Chicago.

Chicago Joe
(Montana Historical Society)

Josephine joined the *demimonde* society. She was hard-working and made good money as a prostitute. Still, she wanted something more. She decided to take her business sense to the gold mining town of Helena, Montana.

A smart business woman herself, Josephine could see there was money just waiting to be made in Helena. She bought a piece of property on Wood Street.

It was only a crude, one-story *hurdy-gurdy* house. It proved so profitable that three years later, Josephine needed to expand, but she would have to borrow money to enlarge her business.

She ended up borrowing from Alex Lavenberg, one of Helena's most notorious lenders, even though the conditions he stipulated were hard to meet.

"Josephine Airey had mortgaged everything, including her underwear—*three dozen pair (of) underclothes,*" wrote Paula Petrik in *Capitalists with Rooms.*

She needn't have worried. Her new venture was so successful that she paid Lavenberg off six months before her note was due.

Helena was literally burned to the ground in 1874. Few of the landowners had money to rebuild. Josephine purchased their property and by the time she was thirty-years-old, she was the largest land owner on Wood Street.

Four years later, Josephine married James T. "Black Hawk" Hensley. They built a fireproof dance hall and "The Red Light Saloon". She rented out her other properties, becoming an influential landlady in Helena.

She also acquired the nickname of "Chicago Joe". She had little trouble operating her Red Light Saloon and managing her "ladies" until 1886, when the city fathers barred prostitution in the city. They also declared hurdy-gurdy houses immoral.

Chicago Joe challenged the city fathers. She hired an attorney who defended her with a few brilliant words and a dictionary. Her attorney read the description of a hurdy-gurdy from his dictionary.

It read that a hurdy-gurdy was a mechanical device that resembled a hand organ. Since the Red Light Saloon had a three-piece band supplying its music, the case was thrown out of court. Chicago Joe was able to keep her Red Light Saloon open.

Joe then built an even more stylish building called the Coliseum. It was a combination theater and variety house. Chicago Joe imported fresh, feminine talent from the east for her new establishment.

The coliseum became the most popular place in Helena. Prostitution and raucous amusement brought in a handsome profit. Here, an eager gentleman could order a fast drink, as well as a fast woman, all on one bill.

According to Rex C. Meyers, writing in Montana Magazine, Chicago Joe paid taxes on more than two-hundred-thousand-dollars worth of property. Her weekly payroll was one thousand dollars or more.

The good life did not last. The Coliseum lost its novelty and the 1893 financial panic and eventual depression put an end to the lavish income of Chicago Joe.

Josephine eventually lost everything, except for the Red Light Saloon. She and her husband moved into an apartment above the saloon and lived quietly.

Chicago Joe died October 25, 1899 of pneumonia.

Chapter 23

Seattle Gets a Bordello

It was the first bawdy house owned by a white man that was stocked with Indian women.

When John Pinnell opened his *Illahee* bordello in Seattle, Washington Territory in 1861, there were few women there other than Indian women. Illahee is a Chinook Indian word meaning *Home Place.*

Seattle was a rough logging town, and the men obviously wanted entertainment other than splitting logs.

Pinnell was already the owner of several lucrative brothels in San Francisco. The bawdy

Indian girls were the only females to work the bordello.

(Google Images)

house marked the beginning of Seattle as a wide-open town, opening it to saloons, brothels, and gambling houses for years to come.

Gary and Gloria Meier, in their book, *Ladies of the Old Northwest,* wrote:

> "Soon after his arrival, John built a large rectangular building of rough boards, housing a dance floor, a long bar, and a number of small private rooms where the primary business would be conducted."

The 1870 Washington census of King County designated the prostitutes working at the Illahee thusly: "Occupied by Indian women kept by one John Pinnell as Hurdie-Gurdies".

A few years later, Pinnell imported a dozen *filles de joie* from San Francisco. They stepped off the boat and headed for the Illahee.

Chapter 24

Trouble in Paradise

Around the time of World War II, Honolulu madams sent mail orders to San Francisco and elsewhere to obtain prostitutes.

According to the Hawaiian Historical Society, in a series called *Chinatown Essays,* the going rates were five-hundred-dollars to one-thousand-dollars, depending on the girl's age. A detective met the steamer off port and herded the girls to a receiving station.

There, the Honolulu vice squad laid down the rules and regulations. Then the girls were taken to the police department for fingerprints and photos.

With this done, the newly-arrived girls were off to work in whichever brothels they were assigned to work their shifts—usually from 1 p.m. to 5 a.m. They were given one day off each week.

"The girls could stay in Honolulu for six months," according to the Chinatown Essays, but then they had to return to the mainland for at least a year.

A noted Honolulu travel writer of the 1930s, Harry A. Franck, commented there were eighteen unlicensed and "officially non-existent hotels and rooming houses," each harboring from six to ten inmates from the mainland.

Honolulu swarmed with servicemen in the war years.
(Google Images)

Honolulu in the 1934 era had a large proportion of "unattached men", the historical society noted. There were twenty-thousand unmarried military and between sixty and seventy thousand Filipinos.

It was felt it was better to have this substitute for true love regulated than unregulated. The *Paradise of the Pacific* magazine urged the city to lay off and let the police do the regulating.

Victor S.K. Houston, a former Hawaii delegate to Congress, in 1941 wanted to close down all the Hawaiian bordellos. At this time military and imported workers totaled an estimated fifty thousand, Houston said.

"The utter absurdity of 203 women servicing fifty-thousand-odd men is evidence on its face," Houston said, noting the influx of even more military after the war started, meant that Honolulu's prostitutes were servicing one-hundred men each day.

This, he said, was a feat that put them in the neighborhood of the British Royal Air Force extolled by Winston Churchill when he said, "Never have so many owed so much to so few."

Hawaii had a real problem in Wahiawa, near Schofield Barracks. Two brothels operated within three doors of the community's school.

Men waiting their turn roamed all over, and often asked school kids for directions. There were cases of indecent exposure.

When children wanted to know why so many people went into and out of these houses, and what they did there, it taxed parental inventiveness.

Because of this, fifty property owners petitioned for relief. At least one brothel was closed following the petition.

Reports claimed that prostitutes in Honolulu earned an average of around twenty-five thousand dollars per year, and many madams earned as much as one hundred fifty thousand dollars per year.

Madam Jean O'Hara said, "Honolulu has always proved a veritable gold mine for the prostitutes and the madams." She said one prostitute had paid her sixty-thousand-dollars for her house, but in little more than a year, owned one-hundred-thousand-dollars worth of Waikiki property and an equal amount in jewels.

Customers paid three-dollars for three-minutes, and the madam took one-dollar off the top. The prostitute had to pay room, board, and laundry out of her two-dollars.

When the police raided several of the houses, one girl said, "I see here from this paper that we can't practice prostitution any more. Heck, I don't practice, I'm an expert."

Chapter 25

The Stingaree District

The Stingaree District in San Diego lay between the wharf and the main business district, catering to sailors as well as businessmen. By the year 1900, its borders stretched for about fifteen blocks. Saloons and dance halls thrived in the Stingaree district.

A stout and bearded Alonzo Horton, 54, arrived in San Diego from San Francisco. After looking over Old Town, he decided the best place for the city to develop is down by the waterfront.

Alonzo Horton
(Google Images)

Horton purchased at auction some eight-hundred-acres of land on the waterfront for approximately 33 cents an acre (some historians credit Horton with paying 27 cents an acre). Two years later, he paid four-thousand-dollars for a one-hundred-sixty acre parcel needed to sew up the section known as the Horton Addition.

Horton built a wharf at the foot of Fifth Avenue at a cost of about fifty-thousand-dollars. It made Fifth Avenue and adjacent streets the backbone of the fast-growing San Diego.

In the 1880s, San Diego became a boomtown. When the gold mines in the Julian area of San Diego County were emptied of their valuable ore, the boom was over. High-priced land that had been keenly sought after by buyers became difficult to sell.

It was in 1887 that call girl Ida Bailey took up residence in a brothel in the Stingaree. The Gaslamp Quarter was known as the Stingaree because it was said you could get stung just as badly in the District as you could by the stingrays in Mission Bay.

An estimated three-hundred-and-fifty prostitutes worked the one-hundred-and-twenty bordellos in the Stingaree District. There were seventy one saloons, carrying such names as the Turf, Oasis, First and Last Chance, Old Tub of Blood, and Legal Tender.

In 1912, police arrested one-hundred-thirty-eight prostitutes in the *Stingaree Raids*. With the red lights officially turned off, San Diego became an unpopular town for the liberty-bound sailors.

When asked to vote for their favorite liberty port, seventeen-hundred-and-ninety men aboard several warships chose San Francisco. San Diego received only seventeen votes.

Police raids had the opposite of the desired effect. Instead of reducing the number of prostitutes as intended, it merely pushed them out into the business district, attracted by the saloons in the Horton Plaza.

In a raid conducted August 19, 1912, Patrolman

The Horton Plaza in late 1800s was the heart of the Gaslamp district.
(San Diego Historical Society)

Pierre Boisseree found four men with Mamie Johnson, Beatrice Smith and others unknown at 439 Second Street. He ordered the women to close the premises.

He returned at 11 p.m. and found the women again engaged with men and arrested them. They were fined thirty dollars each with a six-month suspended sentence on condition they leave town.

On September 13th, Officer Boisseree arrested Julia Barton, the landlady of Canary Cottage, at 4th and J Streets. She was charged with vagrancy and ordered to leave town. Several other arrests were made suggesting that police were attempting to control the Stingaree.

While they might have chased a few women from the district, more than one-hundred-forty prostitutes remained to ply their trade.

By early 1912, pressure to close the Stingaree District had reached its zenith—the city fathers could no longer ignore the problem. Led by Dr. Charlotte Baker, a physician and women's rights leader, members of the WCTU, local clergy, and Door of Hope officials, the committee forced city officials to act.

Police were ordered to round up the women and kick them out of the Stingaree District. Police Chief Keno Wilson said:

"When all is said and done, these women are still women. They are outcasts, but not criminals, and while I will do my duty, I do not propose that this order shall work any unnecessary hardship upon them."

The women were interviewed and asked if they wanted help to "reform".

Clara Doe said she began her career when she was fifteen-years-of-age. After fifteen years, she said she had no regrets.

Flora West said she was twenty-eight-years-old and would be glad to quit the sporting life if she could find a way to do it. She said she could not find work that would pay enough to support her crippled mother and younger sister.

One unnamed prostitute said, "I would like to be good again, but the world won't let me. It must keep me as I am. Please don't say any more. God! Don't I know? Haven't I tried?"

In an attempt to clean up San Diego, the Vice Suppression Commission was created to help rehabilitate prostitutes and help them transition into a life outside of the brothels.

Only two women accepted help from the Vice Suppression Commission. The rest agreed to leave town the next day.

Chapter 26

Dueling Bawdy Girls

El Paso was booming, and two of its most prominent parlor house madams were raging at each other.

No one seems to know when the enmity began. In fact, some surmise they might even have been friends at one time.

Madam Etta Clark was petite and about five foot tall, but she had a big temper. Her temper was so vile it drove away some customers from her Utah Street brothel.

In his book, *The Gentlemen's Club: The Story of Prostitution in El Paso,* author Gordon H. Frost said there was a "plethora of sinners", including prostitutes that arrived in El Paso by train. These women were in need of money and a fresh life.

El Paso's vice zones were the home to gamblers and prostitutes. The zones were collectively known as the "Tenderloin District", and they included East Overland, Oregon, Third and Utah streets.

In the parlor houses, which catered to wealthier clients, the charge to be with a girl was from three-to-five dollars. The lower class crib girls charged fifty-cents to a dollar for their time.

Frost noted that madams knew how to make money off their girls. They charged the girls for the use of the brothel rooms, meals and laundry. Many of the girls were unable to save any money and fell into arrears. The madams then allowed the girls to charge what they owed.

When the girls couldn't pay their debts, madams like Etta Clark would confiscate the girl's belongings until they were repaid.

In El Paso, however, some of Etta Clark's girls decided to sue the madam. Eight of her parlor girls filed suit against Etta, who entered her name in the 1901 Worley's Directory of the City of El Paso as "owner of furnished rooms". She entered her name as Madam Etta Clark

Across the street was Madam "Fat Alice" Abbott, who was the first to build her brothel on Utah street. Fat Alice was six-feet-tall and weighed two-hundred pounds.

Etta Clark and Alice Abbott were business rivals in every sense of the word, although some believe they at one time were friendly.

Alice Abbot had a picture of Etta Clark in her photo album, albeit an arrow with its path directly into Etta's heart was drawn on the photo. Next to the arrow were the words, "Hore to Nigers", the ultimate insult of that prejudiced period.

When Bessie Colvin, one of Alice's girls, left her parlor to work for Etta Clark, Alice tore across the street and banged the door with her fists. When Etta finally opened the door, Alice punched her in the face.

Etta ran to get a gun. She fired a bullet that went straight to Alice's pubic arch.

Clasping her groin, Alice screamed, "My God! I'm shot!" She staggered down the steps and collapsed in the street.

The affair amused El Paso residents as they envisioned the tiny Etta Clark firing a bullet into the most delicate area of Alice Abbott.

Alice survived the shooting. *The El Paso Herald* aptly headline the event as "The Pubic Arch Shooting." The newspaper erred in its attempt at frivolity, however, by misspelling the headline, calling it the "Public Arch Shooting".

It took a jury only fifteen minutes to find Etta Clark not guilty on grounds of self-defense.

The battle between the parlor house madams didn't end there. On July 12, 1888, a fire broke out in Etta's parlor while the women inside were asleep. While the women all escaped unharmed, the fire destroyed the house.

It was later determined that the fire was set by some drunks hired by Fat Alice. Because of a lack of evidence, Alice was acquitted.

Still, the fire put Etta on the street with no place to go. One of her better clients, J.P. Dieter, built her a new place. Dieter's wife was so incensed she divorced him and moved back east with her children.

Dieter and Clark lived together as husband and wife, but never married.

Her new three-story brothel had thirty-two rooms, two parlors, a huge dining area, a ballroom and many bedrooms, and cost Dieter more than one-hundred-twenty-five-thousand dollars to build and furnish.

Fat Alice Abbot retired from the brothel business in 1890, leasing her establishment to Tillie Howard. Alice spent her last years as a very lonely woman. She died in 1896 from a heart attack.

Etta Clark had another house fire at her place, one in which she nearly died. She suffered severe complications from smoke inhalation. On a trip to visit her sister in Atlanta, Etta died of these complications.

Chapter 27

Polygamy and Prostitution

Despite its Mormon religion, Utah didn't escape prostitution.

Mormon leaders loudly protested prostitution, while anti-Mormons accused the polygamous Mormons of practicing a form of prostitution themselves.

With the arrival of the railroad, along with gold miners and the military, Utah Territory received hundreds of women in Salt Lake City that began to sell sex for a living. A few earned small fortunes, according to Jeffery Nichols, author of *Prostitution, Polygamy and Power: Salt Lake City, 1847-1918*.

Author Nichols wrote, "Mormons defended their marital practices as a preservation of women's purity and the sanctity of the family. Mormons, in turn, accused anti-Mormons of hypocrisy for attacking polygamy while tacitly accepting and even supporting prostitution in Salt Lake City."

Non-Mormon women, particularly, denounced plural marriage as a double standard that favored men.

Stockade crib rows in Salt Lake City, 1908.
(Utah Historical Quarterly)

Gentiles viewed polygamy as "sanctified sexual excess" rather than the observance of a sacred principle. To illustrate the point, it is noted that the Church's enemies engaged prostitutes to entice Church leaders, hoping to catch them in verifiable sexual sin, and thus buttress their argument that polygamy was, after all, all about sex.

Author Nichols, claims that at the root of the argument, it is all about power, and who would control Salt Lake City, the Mormons, or the Gentiles.

Nichols wrote, "Prostitution had additional meanings and uses within the Mormon-gentile conflict. For many Mormon men, the presence of women selling sex was a galling symptom of their failure to maintain exclusive control over the city."

Jami Balls, writes in *Utah History to Go,* a website, about the history of the Stockade and Salt Lake City's red light district.

"The general feeling at the beginning of the 20th Century it (prostitution) was considered necessary evil that could never be eliminated, but merely controlled."

Belle London, Madame of the Stockade.
(Utah Historical Quarterly)

In the 1870s, Commercial Street was the center of the red-light district. Parlor houses along the street housed legitimate businesses; usually liquor or tobacco stores, and hel "female boarders" in the upper parts of the houses.

Police regularly conducted raids of these establishments, fining, arresting, and even sometimes conducting physical examinations of the women.

By 1908, a formal registration system existed

where police kept track of the names and addresses of the madams and their houses and in turn, the madam supplied current lists of their girls. Each month, the girls paid a ten-dollar fine which supplied much of the city's revenues.

City fathers didn't like the red light district being so close to its main business district. It adopted a "stockade" policy in1908. Salt Lake City Mayor John Bransford, declared at the time, "I propose to take these women from the business section of the city and put them in a district which will be one of the best, if not the very best, regulated district in the country."

The city brought in Utah's most notorious madam, Belle London, to run the stockade. The stockade consisted of nearly one-hundred small brick "cribs" which were ten feet square, with a door and window, and built in rows.

Girls paid four dollars a day for their "residence". The stockade had three entrances, each guarded to keep both children and undesirable guests from entering, as well as to warn of the periodic police raids.

On September 28, 1911, without explaining why, Belle London announced, "The stockade will be closed on Thursday and the same will not be reopened again."

Some women accepted the offers from the Women's Rescue Station to leave their lives of sin, while others returned to Commercial Street, which continued to be a red light district until the 1930s.

Chapter 28

The Arm of the Law

Prostitution regulation wasn't just a problem for the gold camps and cowtowns of the old west. Officials across the country are still attempting to regulate and clean up red light operations in the modern west.

For instance, surrogate motherhood as a prostitution service was addressed. "If a man's wife has borne him no children, but a prostitute has borne him children, he shall provide for that prostitute wine, oil and clothing and the children which the prostitute has borne him shall be his heirs but as long as the wife lives, the prostitute shall not abide in the house with the wife."

Wives were confined to domestic activities and not permitted to socialize outside. In this structure, women who were not model wives were not able to support themselves except through prostitution, so a large prostitution economy developed.

According to Judith Walkowitz, author of Prostitution in Victorian Society, (Cambridge University Press, 1980) "Many women, who did not have sexually transmitted diseases when they were arrested, got them from the unsterile, newly invented speculums used to examine them."

The Record, by Priscilla Alexander 1994, indicates the majority of prostitutes can not work in legally specified ways, so that most of prostitution is criminalized. For example, in most legalized systems of prostitution only ten to twenty percent of prostitutes comply with regulation, including 'Registration, Mandatory Testing and Health Certificates.

The Council For Prostitution Alternatives, issued a 1991-92 survey of fifty-five street prostitutes in Portland, Oregon. Fifty-five percent said they were the victims of sexual torture.

For example, a woman from the Philippines reported being offered a job in a hotel in Europe by a high government official. She was not a prostitute at the time, and no mention was made of sex.

After much indecision, she decided to go. When she arrived, she found that the job was in fact prostitution, and that she had no choice in the matter.

Laws against 'traffic' in women, which are supposed to prevent the forced movement of women and girls across national or state boundaries for the purposes of prostitution are, instead, used to keep voluntary prostitutes from traveling.

The White Slave Traffic Act, introduced in 1910 (also known as the Mann Act) was the first glaring example of racist results of the misdirected attempts to deal with sexual slavery.

The first prominent person charged was Jack Johnson, the First Black Heavyweight champion, who had an affair with, and eventually married, a white prostitute. He was charged under the act, and convicted of transporting her across a state line.

Johnson's story is interesting from a racial aspect as well. Johnson, born in Galveston, Texas, in 1878, started boxing as a teen in the Jim Crow era. African-Americans were permitted to compete for most titles, but not for heavyweight champion of the world.

But Johnson kept challenging heavyweight champ James J. Jeffries, who refused to fight him and retired undefeated. In 1908, though, the new champion, Tommy Burns, agreed to fight Johnson in Australia (lured by the then princely sum of $30,000).

Johnson won, becoming the first African-American heavyweight champion of the world. His victory spurred a frantic search for a "great white hope" to win back the title.

Ultimately, Burns agreed to come out of retirement to fight Johnson, on July 4, 1910, in Reno, Nev. At the end of that fight, dubbed "the battle of the century," Burns was a bloody mess—the footage is almost painful to watch and Johnson was still the champ.

This time, his win sparked nationwide race riots and shocking racist editorials in venerable newspapers. The sight of a black man beating a white man was considered so incendiary that

Congress eventually banned the interstate transport of fight films.

Further incensing the white community, and eventually even African-Americans, was Johnson's refusal to keep a low profile. He wore flamboyant clothes, drove expensive cars and consorted with white women, mostly prostitutes.

Eventually, Johnson married a white woman, Etta Duryea, but he also had extramarital affairs, drank heavily and sometimes abused Duryea. Duryea, who suffered from depression, committed suicide in 1912.

Though said to be grief-stricken, Johnson married another white woman, former prostitute Lucille Cameron, three months later.

Though their relationship was consensual, the government charged Johnson with violating the Mann Act, passed in 1910, which outlawed the interstate transport of women "for the purpose of prostitution, debauchery or for any other immoral purpose."

Sentenced to a year in prison, Johnson fled the country and spent several years as a fugitive in Europe and Mexico. In 1915, he lost his title to Jess Willard in a match in Cuba.

Six years later, Johnson returned to the United States and served his time in prison. He died at age 68 in 1946 from injuries suffered in a traffic accident in North Carolina, shortly after he'd been forced to eat at the back of a diner.

Chapter 29

Attempts at Control

> "Why should it be illegal to sell something that is perfectly legal to give away."
>
> George Carlin

Attempts to control prostitution began as early as the sixteenth century in Europe. Sexually transmitted disease was rampant, so brothels were closed throughout western and central Europe.

Strict punishment was handed out to those engaged in the trade. When punishment failed to curb the disease, some cities instituted even stricter controls. Berlin required medical inspection in 1700; Paris began to register its prostitutes in 1785.

Great Britain enacted a series of *Contagious Diseases Prevention Acts*. These acts required periodic medical examination of all prostitutes in military and naval districts and the detention of all of those found to be infected.

These acts failed to curb the sexual diseases and the laws were repealed in 1886.

In 1898, Great Britain enacted the *Vagrancy Act*, which prohibited males from living on the earning of prostitutes.

Internationally, efforts were made to control the traffic of women for the purpose of prostitution. This effort began in 1899 with a congress in London. Other conferences followed, in Amsterdam in 1901, London, 1902, and Paris in 1904.

The League of Nations, in 1919, appointed an official body to gather all facts pertaining to the trafficking of prostitutes. And, in 1921, a conference held in Geneva, and attended by thirty-four countries, established the Committee on the Traffic of Women and Children.

In the United States, there was no effort to stamp out prostitution until the end of the nineteenth century. In 1910, The Mann Act, or White Slave Traffic Act, was passed. The act forbade the interstate and international transportation of women for immoral purposes.

By 1915, nearly all of the states had passed laws regarding the keeping of brothels or profiting in other ways from the earnings of prostitutes.

Still, during World War I, there was a great increase in prostitution, accompanied by an increase in sexually transmitted disease.

Now, all states except Nevada have legislation that makes it a crime to operate a house of prostitution.

In 1883, sociologist Joel Best wrote a book on prostitution in St. Paul, Minnesota, in an attempt to examine the experience of prostitution in a middle-sized city.

"St. Paul appears to be neither exceptionally corrupt nor exceptionally virtuous by late nineteenth-century standards," according to Best's research. At the same time, Best seemed to feel there is little to be done to totally wipe out prostitution.

In ancient times, according to *The Free Dictionary*, by Farlex, a website, prostitution in some instances, had religious connotations. "Sexual intercourse with temple maidens was an act of worship to the temple deity."

In Greece the *hetaerae (Gr.,=* companions or associates) were often women of high social status. In Rome, the *meretrices* were on the low social level and were forced to wear wigs and special garments signifying their trade.

In the middle ages, prostitution flourished, and licensed brothels were a source of revenue to the municipalities.

In some Muslim countries, prostitution carries a death penalty, while in other countries, prostitutes are tax-paying and sometimes even unionized. In the Netherlands, prostitution is legal and can even be advertised, although the prostitutes themselves must be at least eighteen-years-of-age.

There are many people that would agree with comedian George Carlin, "Why should it be illegal to sell something that's perfectly legal to give away."

Index

About the Author

Alton Pryor has been a writer for magazines, newspapers, and wire services. He worked for United Press International in their Sacramento Bureau, handling both printed press as well as radio news.

He moved to Salinas, where he worked for the Salinas Californian daily newspaper for five years as editor of Western Ranch and Home, a weekend supplement.

In 1963, he joined California Farmer magazine where he was a staff writer for 27 years. When that magazine

Alton Pryor

sold, the magazine's writers were let go. Alton then pursued freelancing, and gained an intense interest in California and Western history after selling ten short 500-word articles on Southern California history.

In his research of these stories, he found other stories that interested him but did not fit the publication for whom he wrote. He collected the facts and ideas as he researched, and finally turned them into his first book, "Little Known Tales in California History."

He is a graduate of California State Polytechnic University, San Luis Obispo, where he earned a Bachelor of Science degree in journalism.

179

Stagecoach Publishing

5360 Campcreek Loop
Roseville, CA 95747
1-800-591-3618   916-771-8166
stagecoach@surewest.net
www.stagecoachpublishing.com

Quantity	Title	Retail Cost
	California's Hidden Gold	11.95
	Classic Tales in CA. History	11.95
	Cowboys, The End of the Trail	11.95
	Fascinating Women in California History	11.95
	Historic California	11.95
	Jonathan's Red Apple Tree	3.95
	Little Known Tales in California History	11.95
	Publish It Yourself	9.95
	Outlaws and Gunslingers	11.95
	The Lawmen	11.95
	Little Known Tales in Hawaii History	11.95
	Little Known Tales in Nevada History	11.95
	The Bawdy House Girls of the Old West	11.95
	The Timeless Quotations of President Ronald Reagan	6.95
	Those Wild and Lusty Gold Camps	11.95
S & H: $3 for first book, plus $1 for ea additional book		
	Total Shipping Charges:	
	Total	

Credit Card #

Expiration Date: Telephone #:

Name:

Address:

Signature